Women and Depression

Women and Depression

Edited by

Iffat Hussain

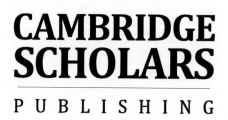

CAMBRIDGE
SCHOLARS

PUBLISHING

Women and Depression, Edited by Iffat Hussain

This book first published 2010

Cambridge Scholars Publishing

12 Back Chapman Street, Newcastle upon Tyne, NE6 2XX, UK

British Library Cataloguing in Publication Data
A catalogue record for this book is available from the British Library

ISBN (10): 1-4438-2114-4, ISBN (13): 978-1-4438-2114-8

CONTENTS

FOREWORD

IFFAT HUSSAIN

According to the World Health Organisation (WHO), "depression is not only the most common women's mental health problem, but may be more persistent in women than men."[1] The WHO has estimated that by the year 2020, depression will be the second most common disability causing disease in the world.

Depression is complex in relation to other symptoms. It falls in various categories: it may be a psychiatric illness, a syndrome, a symptom, a sustained change in affect, or a transient mood. When it is excessive and persistent and may result in a loss of contact with reality, then it is considered a psychiatric disorder.

The symptoms and diagnosis of depression are more prevalent in women than in men. The evidence shows that depressed individuals are less productive than non-depressed individuals, and throughout the world, rates of depression are greater among females than males. Depression is an illness in which symptoms are primarily physical and psychological with more adverse and distressing complaints. This leads to impairment of work capacity, reduction and lessening of social functioning, the suffering of patients' families if the disorder is prolonged.

This book, *Depression and Women*, is a collection of researched papers and essays from authors, produced in the hope that it will encourage a comprehensive understanding of this condition which is so common among women, and that it will provide an insight into depression to a wide variety of professionals and people outside the medical field. The chapters show different aspects of the phenomenon, taking a broad view of the subject of depression in women. There is also a concentration on interpersonal therapy and counselling for depressive conditions. These

---

[1] World Health Organisation, Preamble to the Constitution of the World Health Organization as adopted by the International Health Conference, New York, 19–22 June, 1946; signed on 22 July 1946 by the representatives of 61 States (Official Records of the World Health Organization, no. 2, p. 100) and entered into force on 7 April 1948.

essays are not purely "medically" based: it is also intended to be accessible to those outside the medical field: patients, their families and friends and anyone who is interested in or curious about this condition.

This edited volume on women and depression is multidisciplinary, including cultural, sociological, public health, psychology and psychiatry aspects. As the origins of depression are various and result in a high prevalence of depression in women, this book may lead to further interdisciplinary views on women and depression. I believe that the more we learn, the greater the probability that we can eradicate the debilitating nature of depression in the near future.

Most of the authors contributing to this book *Women and Depression* are women; they have all communicated their professional experience, information and knowledge to make this a valuable book. *Women and Depression* integrates the latest information from women experts in fields including sociology, psychology, psychiatry and public health to address issues concerning depression.

I hope that this book will provide useful information concerning depression in women and also as a paragon for continued international and interdisciplinary research.

I wish success and blissful life to all the women who are suffering from depression, and that those who are beginning their fight against this illness do not let it come between them and a a life full of joy and happiness. I look forward joining them on the path to better and happy lives.

I am very grateful to and appreciative of all the authors who have communicated their valuable work in *Women and Depression*, with the aim to benefit and make this world a joyous place for women with depression. Their work in this book is summarized below.

In "Showing One's Sadness in a Visual Context: Providing a Sense of Community and Support for Depressed Women through Video Interviews," Dr. Irmeli Laitinen and Professor Elizabeth Ettorre report the findings from forty-eight video interviews used in the Women and Depression Project (WDP) in Finland (Laitinen, 2008; Laitinen & Ettorre, 2004, 2007; Laitinen, Ettorre, & Sutton, 2006, 2007). The video work used in this project incorporates narrative interviews and is embedded in oralysis. Videos provide participants with mirror images of themselves: with this the researchers and participants developed short-term, therapeutic interventions in order to provide a sense of community and support for marginalised, depressed women. Dr. Laitinen and Professor Ettore also generated an action-research approach for depressed women and gathered valuable data concerning women's experiences of depression.

In their essay "The Role of Community-Based Groups in the Prevention and Recovery of Postnatal Depression," Shari Read and Debra Rickwood examine the role of group membership with regard to positive mental-health outcomes for women with young children. Specifically, they explore whether community-based groups provide aspects of prevention and health promotion in supporting otherwise isolated stay-at-home mums with young children. The research employed a questionnaire-based survey of three groups of women: those who participate in a community-based women's group, women who participate in one of a number of ACT playgroups, and stay-at-home mums who were not participating in a parenting-related community group at the time of the research. Analysis compared each of the research groups on measures of social-connectedness, group-belonging and support, resilience and postnatal depression.

Dr Tracie O'Keefe illustrates four women's cases in "Overcoming Depression and Female Learned Helplessness through Hypnotherapy," describing how they were able to overcome their depression by learning a greater sense of self-efficacy during hypnotherapy. These four women were helped in relation to a sense of depression through hypnotherapeutic intervention and personality alteration. In their own way, they suffered from low self-esteem and poor self-image: this is a common theme found among women who suffer from depressive states for extended periods of time beyond the norm, due to patriarchal cultural ideations.

Kim Davis is a Dru yoga therapist. In her essay she explores why yoga is one of the fastest-growing self-help modalities today—particularly among women suffering depression. Kim discusses the internationally researched evidence supporting the value of yoga in the treatment of depression and explains the specific value of Dru yoga for transforming negative emotional states through gentle therapeutic movements, breathing, positive guided imagery and affirmation.

Dr. Sabin Sabin Fernbacher and Christine Hodge argue in their essay "Childhood Sexual Abuse and Depression—Connections, Theories and Practice Implications within the Primary Care Setting," that primary-care providers often work with women who suffer from depression, but they are not always aware of their clients' history of childhood sexual abuse. They look at this issue and some of the tensions concerning this area of work, such as screening for childhood sexual abuse—"to ask or not to ask"—during the assessment phase. Furthermore, they discuss dilemmas and organisational processes that need to be considered if such inquiry is to be made routine.

In "Depression in African Women," Magnolia Bahle Ngcobo and

Professor Basil J Pillay studied depression in African women attending a health service. Clinical records of female patients presenting with depression at a General Hospital in a densely populated African township were examined over a two-year period. A review of the biographical and epidemiological data of these patients is presented. Depression in these women was related to socioeconomic factors such as poverty, overcrowding, unemployment, high levels of crime, and lack of services and abuse to a considerable degree a relic of the past discriminatory apartheid system.

Iffat Hussain explains the psychological effects and depression in women who are forced to wear veils in "Forced Muslim Religious Seclusion and Veiling for Women and Depression." She comments on this misconception of Islamic practice: the religious seclusion and veiling propagated and preached by Muslim fundamentalists result in a very vulnerable and powerless position for women in the society and in turn may result in depression for women. She explains effects and symptoms of depression these women may show. In addition she adds quotes and complaints of the women against forced veiling and seclusion.

Arts Therapist Belinda Cody presents the case study of a female client who experienced multiple losses following several consecutive significant bereavements. Underlying factors eventually precipitated the onset of a complex period of chronic ill-health and disability, leading to depression. As an alternative to pharmaceutical solutions, the client chose to engage in a range of therapies, according to her needs, from both conventional and emerging therapeutic paradigms.

Nancy Moodley and Professor Basil J Pillay present their paper, "Depression in Female Spinal Cord Injured Patients." Their study examines the patients admitted to a provincial spinal rehabilitation unit over the course of one year, most of whom were paraplegic. A semi-structured interview and the Beck's Depression Inventory (BDI) were administered. This study suggests that spinal-cord-injured women experience many losses after the injury and are at a great risk of suffering from depression.

Karen Noonan and Isabelle Ellis write about depression as a symptom of the rare medical condition porphyria. Karen Noonan was herself diagnosed with this condition and discusses her experience of having this disease. Porphyria has been linked with depression and it is said that women display symptoms three times more often than males. The other cases mentioned highlight the fact that this disease is often mis- and under-diagnosed.

In "The Missing Link: Women, Depression and Midlife Transition,"

Robyn Vickers-Willis draws on Jungian psychology and her own research on midlife development to explain why midlife is a time of significant psychological and spiritual development for a woman, a time when it is vital for her to embrace her feelings rather than sedate or run away from them if she is to create a personally meaningful second half of life. The essay also considers the impact of the omission of context from much of the current thinking on depression and the role the language of depression plays in women's midlives.

Professor Carolyn Quadrio explains different dimensions of depression in "Psychiatry and Depressed Women," which may be biogenetic, psychological and socio-cultural, and gives multidimensional analysis and reasons explaining why depression is more common in women than men. She provides an overview of factors such as trauma and abuse, biogenetic factors, socio-cultural, political, and economic factors, and psychological factors. She argues that focusing on the relationship of depression to reproductive functions diverts attention from the universal realities of women's lives.

Thank You,

—Iffat Hussain
February 2010

SHOWING ONE'S SADNESS IN A VISUAL CONTEXT: PROVIDING A SENSE OF COMMUNITY AND SUPPORT FOR DEPRESSED WOMEN THROUGH VIDEO INTERVIEWS

IRMELI LAITINEN AND ELIZABETH ETTORRE

Introduction

Depression is a multidimensional, multicultural phenomenon (Bhui & Olajide, 1999; Nazaroo, 1997). To fully understand the embodied material, subjective and discursive aspects of experiences labelled as depression demands drawing upon knowledge that is interdisciplinary (Stoppard, 1997) and sensitive to cultural diversity. The need to recognise the challenge of cultural diversity when analysing depression is important, as emphasised by Falicov (2003), who contends that in contrast to an epidemiological or biomedical approach, a cultural, "ethnographic" one allows us to study the experiences labelled as depression in each society with its own beliefs and meaning systems. Western constructions of depression vary and can be viewed as locally constructed and dependent upon circumstances and environment as well as other social factors.

The purpose of this paper is to report on findings from forty-eight video interviews used in the Women and Depression Project (WDP) in Finland (See Laitinen, 2008; Laitinen & Ettorre, 2004, 2007; Laitinen, Ettorre & Sutton, 2006, 2007). While some may argue that the video could do for psychology and the social sciences what the microscope has done for medicine (Biggs, 1983: 91), the use of videos can be seen as a *bona fide* qualitative research method (Loizos, 2000). The technique of video recording is quite common in therapeutic settings (Rennie, 1994; Angus & Rennie, 1989) and in these settings a video allows a patient to observe him/herself as others see them (Hosford & Mills, 1983). It enables patients to learn what they don't know about themselves but what is known to others (McCrea, 1983: 95). Videos provide them with mirror images of themselves.

The video work used in this project incorporates narrative interviews and is embedded in what Ulmer (1989) calls oralysis. For example, as researchers seek new ways of understanding and reporting data, oralysis refers to

> the way in which oral forms, derived from everyday life, are, with the recording powers of video, applied to the analytical tasks associated with literate forms. (Ulmer, 1989: ix)

In oralysis, the traditional product of interviewing, talk, is coupled with the visual, providing a visualised audio product consonant with a society that is dominated by the television medium (Ulmer, 1989).

Videos have been used increasingly as a data-gathering tool in social research (Dowrick & Biggs, 1983; Ball & Smith, 1992; Bauer & Gaskill, 2000; Emmison & Smith, 2000; Harper, 2000; Holliday, 2000). In social research, it has evolved in health services as well as other disciplines (Bottorff, 1994), and has been a useful method for recording human interaction in natural settings (Goodwin, 1993) and in working settings where one observes a web of social interactions and activities (Bodker, 1996). Gilgun (1992) has argued that video recording allows theory-generating processes to develop.

The aim of WDP was threefold: 1) to develop a short-term, therapeutic intervention in order to provide a sense of community and support for marginalised, depressed women; 2) to generate an action research approach for depressed women; and 3) to gather valuable data concerning women's experiences of depression.

Methods

With both therapeutic and research aims, therapy was utilised in group work with depressed women recruited from community settings. The target population was adult women who had defined themselves as being depressed and/or had been treated for clinical depression (i.e. defined by a treater as clinically depressed), and who wanted to participate in ten group meetings with other women who were depressed. Group members were recruited at least two months before a group began, mainly through leaflets advertising the group. Eleven groups were organised in three Finnish cities for five years from 1994 to 1999 and they were held both in public and private health care settings located in urban centres. The final study population consisted of 101 women with an average age of forty.

There were a variety of ways in which both qualitative and quantitative data were collected from members during the group process. These included: a pre-group interview, questionnaire 1 (Q1), health diaries, questionnaire 2 (Q2), first video interview, second video interview, questionnaire 3 (Q3), group leader's narrative accounts and group leader's diary. The rationale for the use of varied data collection techniques was to generate an awareness of the complexities of the group process and to ensure that a multi-level approach to data gathering on both an individual and collective level was maintained. Not all methods were used for each group. This was for developmental (i.e. the data collection techniques were being developed at the time and not yet used in a particular group) and logistic (i.e. the first author was not the main facilitator in some groups based outside the original catchment area) reasons. This paper will report only on findings from the video interviews.

Linking a therapeutic program with action research. In action research, the researcher gives results back to service providers. In this type of research, researchers employ a multi-method approach, continually process activities and changes, and document these activities in order to identify issues that might have an impact on service delivery. The first author and main researcher on the WDP developed a process of working within action research which uses criteria such as problem solving, collaboration, participation and self-evaluation. As action research as well as a therapeutic programme, the WDP was flexible and involved a continual evaluation of the therapeutic strategies and research measurements which were used.

The therapeutic programme. WDP offered a time-limited (i.e. ten one hour and forty-five minute group sessions over ten weeks) therapeutic group program for depressed women and included a series of thirty therapeutic exercises. Groups gave members the opportunity to learn communication skills, which helped them to value self-help, mutual support and a sense of themselves as women. While the focus of each session was on a particular topic, self-help techniques were learned through various exercises. Besides the weekly group sessions, a follow-up session was held one year after the group finished. While a therapeutic aim of WDP was to effect positive change with a beneficial impact on women's experience of depression, the purpose of the follow-up was to assess this overall aim by gathering information concerning members' well-being. Two experienced female group leaders led the groups. Prior to participation in the group, the key researcher trained group leaders.

Key therapeutic questions were asked, which included:

- How do depressed women experience depression?

- What kinds of symptoms do they perceive in their lives?
- What life-events, feelings and activities do they link with their depression?
- What kinds of social supports and other forms of treatments (including prescribed drugs) do they encounter while depressed?
- What kinds of changes do they want in their lives?
- Most importantly, is it possible for depressed women who have traditionally been dealt with as objects of treatment to become active subjects in healing their depression?

It was hoped that this research would provide an exploratory method in order to assess whether or not groups are able to help women cope more effectively with depression than if left to their own devices.

Video Interviews

The first author, having used this technique in her family therapy work as a psychotherapist, was quite familiar with video interviews as a therapeutic device. In WDP, video interviews were "normal" psychotherapeutic sessions but ones that were video recorded.

First video interview (45 minutes). A semi-structured interview with active listening techniques, reassurance, feedback (Renne et al., 1983: 31) and free association were used to give space for respondents' own voices. Specific questions asked included:

- How do you understand yourself in your life with your difficulties and your troubles?
- Why do you think you have had to lean on professional helpers?
- What do you think of the help you have had here and earlier?
- Have you ever felt yourself to be depressed, and if yes, what was it like for you?

After these questions, women were free to talk and describe their lives in whatever way they wanted. This interview format allowed a respondent to evaluate her current situation, to consider whether or not herself understanding had changed after her involvement in the WDP group and to discuss what had helped her most. In these interviews, respondents described in their own words their experiences of depression. During this interview the camera was focused on both the respondent and researcher.

Second video interview (5 to 15 minutes). A week after the first interview, the respondent and the researcher watched the first video together. After this viewing, the interviewer asked the respondent how she felt when she was watching the video, and this session was also videoed. In the second recording, the camera was focused on the participant given that she was the only one who gave feedback about the video. The purpose of the second video interview was to give a participant the possibility of seeing herself, her ways of communicating with other people, her communicative style including non-verbal communication (body language, gestures, tone of voice, etc.) and being reflective towards herself.

Sample. Fifty out of 101 respondents had individual video interviews after their group finished, but two of these video interviews failed and were eliminated from the final sample, leaving forty-eight as the total number. These forty-eight respondents who had video interviews were members of five different groups: two groups were in the public sector (n = twenty members) and three groups in the private sector (n = twenty-eight members). Of these forty-eight women, the majority (n = twenty-seven) were working, seven were unemployed and seven were students. Four members were on permanent sick leave, while three were at home. The average age was around forty: eight women were between twenty and twenty-nine, eighteen between thirty and thirty-nine, thirteen women between forty and forty-nine and nine women were between fifty and fifty-nine. Of these forty-eight respondents, three had severe psychiatric problems while ten were having problems coping with their everyday lives.

During the last session of these groups, the group leader gave every group member an envelope, containing notification of the time of her video interview. For the first time since her pre-group interview, the video interview presented the member with an opportunity to have a special therapeutic session with the group leader on her own. Members participated in a video interview at least one to two weeks after the group ended. Here it should be noted that three women were not willing to be recorded by video camera but agreed to be tape-recorded during the time allocated for their video interview.

Data analysis. During the data analysis stage of the research, the author viewed all video interviews twice and some many times in order to register body movements. The relevant interviews were transcribed by the author between November 2000 and March 2001 and key themes were identified. Excerpts from the video interviews will be used in this paper.

Results

First video interview. When members focused on the main problem in their lives (which led them to their depression) in the first video interview, they gave a variety of answers. Four major problems, troubles or worries were mentioned. These included: 1) troubles with a partner or significant other (n = twenty), 2) problems with work or studies (n = sixteen), 3) problems with herself (n = eight) and worries about other family members (n = 4).

1. Troubles with a partner or significant other (n = 20). Four group members reported that there were in the process of having a divorce. One woman had been trying to separate from her husband for years, but in her interview she said: "I am divorcing; it takes all my strength... I can't do it... I am not able to do it" (Arja, forty-three).

So for this woman she is divorcing and not divorcing at the same time. Three members discovered that their husbands had had a relationship with another woman, while four women experienced domestic violence. Those women who discovered that their husbands had a relationship with another woman said:

> [It is an] awful shock to wake up from a daydream and believe that my husband had another woman, his colleague from his work...I am so bitter and angry...I want to kill him, so to speak. (Elina, 17)

and

> After then last couple of years so many things have been cleared up. I have a feeling I have been cheated by him. I took care of that family. He was working but now I know he wasn't always working. He was with another woman. I packed the suitcases for him and ironed his shirts. I was a servant. (Kirsti, 22)

Two of the women who were victims of domestic violence were afraid to tell to their husbands that they were participating in the WDP group. As a result, they were offered a locked file cabinet in which they were able to leave their diaries and other group materials. They said:

> In the beginning it was love...It has lasted now for nine years... He is very demanding and I got beaten up and my sons were not happy about it when they saw me all black and blue... They did not get along, these kids and this man [stepfather]...and I have to be split up in two pieces ...I could not let this relationship go, and of course these boys were very dear to me... (Leila, 47)

and

> I would like to be invisible and as neutral as possible and please everybody like my parents and my husband. So I move along with other people's

needs and on the other hand I am extremely critical and demanding about what concerns me. (Päivi, 20)

Other women who experienced violence in their homes said:

I am very insecure and fearful. I have understood that I have a constant fear...of knives... I don't dare use knives because I have these sorts of feelings. My father used to pretend to do suicide. He was laying on the living room couch and threatened to kill himself with that knife... So I have been living in a miserable situation since my childhood and I have thought many times to kill myself. (Meri, 21)

I am a person that people can manipulate easily. If I have an opinion so I can change my opinions because I am afraid of fights and I give up... My husband is just like my mother. My mother was awful with her mouth, tight with her opinions and had odd rules. (Liisa, 19)

Two women reported that their husbands drank too much alcohol, and for one of these women that was the main reason why they were facing serious economic problems. She said:

This moment is feeling good because I just received a phone call from a bank and we have gave us a new loan... [The] good point is that when you have big financial problems, he does not have money to drink... (Irma, 37)

Other women who reported relationship problems with their partners spoke about lack of commitment and support from partners. Those who were separating from partners had ambivalent relationships with them.

I wanted another child and then my husband said if we do it then you must take care of it totally and then I thought I can't do it...then I was very sad for a long time that I cannot have another child... (Leena, 30)

This above participant was already suffering physical stress symptoms relating to her work and domestic duties.

2. Problems with work or studies (n = 16). Problems concerning work varied for respondents. Three women reported that they were unemployed and had been without work for a number of years. Two of them had had a permanent job (for thirteen and twenty-three years, respectively). However, suddenly these two women had felt that they could not work anymore and left their workplaces. Two other respondents had sought treatment because of the sudden loss of their jobs. Both of them were childless, career women for whom work was an important part of their self-image. They were both over fifty years old and mentioned that it was hard to find new

work if one is over forty. One of the women expressed her despair by saying: "I heard in a Swedish television program that women over fifty are antique" (Leena, 24).

The other woman was a famous personality who had regular appearances on a national television programme. For her, losing her job caused not only self-doubt and self-blame, but also immense shame in front other people—including the Finnish public. Her husband took her to see a psychiatric because she had had serious thoughts of killing herself. During her video interview, this woman said that she had felt too depressed to participate fully in the WDP groups. However, the group had helped her to go out from home to meet people and she could meet her old friends again. Other difficulties with work included a woman who was not satisfied with her job (of more than twenty years) and wanted a change (she had a senior post in the Finnish media).

One woman was experiencing burnout as a result of having an alcohol problem as well as marital problems. Another woman had been on three months' stress leave. She said she was working in a male profession and for much of the time, she felt that she was being excluded from her work mates' conversations. She believed that she was discriminated against as well as overlooked during promotion rounds. Another woman was trying to cope with a difficult boss but felt that she could not manage without the support of professional workers in a psychiatric unit and the WDP group.

One woman was on sick leave after having stressful time in her workplace. She felt that she was incapable of doing her work. Her colleagues isolated her and ignored her. She felt totally disabled in her work. She tried to resolve this work problem by trying to commit suicide:

> If I only think of myself, I am annoyed that I was not successful in that (i.e. suicide) and I am so ashamed and embarrassed that even in that I did not succeed just as in so many other things... (Sirkka, 45)

Seven women had various problems with their studies. Five of these women were talented young students from Helsinki University who had no capacity to enjoy their studies. The main reason why they came to the group was the long waiting lists for individual counselling in the student health service.

3. Problems with herself (n = 8). Eight women felt that their main problems were with themselves. Two women complained of loneliness. One said that she lacked any kind of social skills. Another woman said:

> Already in my teenage years I was terribly lonely and alone, and that's how I never learned how to be social even still I am lacking of basic skills how to approach a person. (Sinikka, 52)

Two women were suffering from severe alcohol problems and this was compounded by the fact that both of their husbands were also alcoholics. One woman's problem was that she was angry all of the time. She said about herself:

> Nothing ever changes. My biggest problem in my life is that I am such a hellishly irritating and peevish, ill-tempered human being that it is limiting my everyday life. I have no strength to be what I should be... [like] some kind of mother figure I have in my mind which I would like to be... but no way this kind of lumberjack which I am. I am not at all like that mother image... I don't have even any kind of ability or resources... (Ritva, 50)

Another woman whose problem with herself was that she heard voices said:

> It was difficult especially when these voices came...I felt all the sins of the humankind...that kind of mental pain you can't imagine. If someone would cut off my hand with an axe, it would not hurt so much as I felt in the forest sitting on a tree stump...It was so painful that there were not many roads...or then a death or something else ... (Irma, 54)

4. Worries about other family members (n = 4). Four women reported that their problems were linked to their worries about other family members. These included worries related to: a member's only child had left for summer camp; a member's children were having psychological problems and the recent suicide of a member's father. The last woman sought help after her father had committed the suicide. Her parents were divorced because her father was an alcoholic. She had found her father dead in his house. She felt guilty and depressed after the incident. She said:

> For a month after my Dad's death, I could not do anything...I just felt very empty. I could hardly wake up in the mornings or take my clothes off when I went to bed I felt so awful. Nothing interested me....Day after day was more awful...I could not go lower...I was eating sleeping pills. I had thoughts about what if something would happen to my car like an accident...I did not think of the future at all...I was stuck with one thing...I was in a prison of my own depression...I could not see anything.... (Helena, 75)

For one member, her husband was constantly moving workplaces in different countries and continents. She tried to raise two children and at the same time, finish her studies at university. Recently, she had been diagnosed with cancer. The cancer had been "cured", but during that time she had not received any psychological support.

The second video interview. The second video interview provided respondents with a new way of seeing themselves and evaluating their lives.

Ritva (29) explained that the reason for her present problems is based on her relationship with her child's father, who has been her boyfriend. She sees herself too dependent on him. The problem lies also on that fact that Ritva wants to have a proper family with this man. She sees things about herself that she had never seen. After Ritva watched her first video interview, she said:

> This video should be shown in a primary school for girls as an example of a warning—as a feminist expression of opinion.... "Don't you girls put yourself in this kind of situation!".... But [still] there was everything in my life, which causes me the problems I have....

Then she says:

> I wonder if it is true what Mikko [her child's father] has said that I somehow enjoy suffering...a professional complainer, as he calls me.

At the end of the second video interview, she says:

> I am tired of it...I don't want to go on and on...and I want to get rid of that what any emotions of it...Once for all there are limits to everything...

She is silent and then she starts:

> But, I must say that in that video (the first video that she just watched) there was everything in a nutshell...all the most important things and what causes these problems...I could see things in myself that I have never seen before...

In her feedback video, Pia (thirty-eight) is livelier than in her first video interview. She uses the feedback video to mirror herself and she makes it clear that she needs another person to talk to about herself. She can't talk to her husband, and when she cannot talk to anybody she feels that her life situation has been more chaotic than she observes now in a video. But when she is analyzing herself and tells about it one cannot be without noticing that she uses passive form when telling about her own life. She wants to be even closer to the interviewer, looks her in the eyes and leans forward, holding her hands on her knees and starts talking after a short silent moment:

> I can see that there is some kind of structure in my life situation. When you are home alone and you don't talk to anybody.... But now when I heard it with my own ears, when I talked here with somebody it feels that there is structure in my life situation and it does not feel so chaotic.... And when one talks to somebody, one notices that some solutions have been made to the one direction or the other.... I could not work at home with my diary...I need people to talk to...I noticed that my life is going awfully lot around my husband.... But this is now in this moment....

Marja (fifty-four) used this video interview to tell the therapist how she has felt earlier and how she feels now. She reflects on her current and past psychological well-being and how she sees herself. She tells about her treatment how she was first disappointed but later found it beneficial. She also tells how she has been depressed and how painful it was for her. She also says that she is happy enough now to enjoy the life and for a long time she has not been happier. Directly after seeing the video, she yawns and smiles and says:

> ...I was actually nervous to come back (and see the video) and in the beginning, it felt really awful but after all, it was fun to look at it.... I thought that it would be much more muddled than it was....

While saying this she waves her hands around in front of her and continues: "...It was so mixed up, but it was all clearly there and one could understand it..." She changes her sitting position to look more assertive, and folds her arms in front of her chest, saying:

> ...I thought to myself that if I would see this woman on television, I would tell her that take yourself by the scruff of your neck and cheer up.... Do something to yourself... [she's] not at all a happy person.... But it is enough for me [in this moment] that I am alive...

She puts her right hand on her chest where about her heart is and says:

> ...I am very satisfied with it [life]...I am able to be satisfied with ordinary life...Like the forest.... Little puddles in the road.... This is my happiest time in my life.... I don't have any pain or anxiety....

She says this with a higher voice, looks at the interviewer straight in her eyes: "...I don't feel awful or depressed.... Even though this may sound [that I was a] very phlegmatic and monotonic person [in that video]...." She nods with her head to the TV monitor and then shows a straight line in front of her with her right hand and lifts her shoulders up: "...but what is healthier than this?" And she smiles at the interviewer.

Helena (25) is young and very conscious of how she looks at herself in her video, reflecting on when she will be older and perhaps wiser, knowing that without any doubt she will be moving on from this moment in her life without knowing yet what direction. She is very optimistic about her future. She did experience a deep depression after her father's death, and now she is satisfied that she is over it. In the group, she could learn a new, more accepting attitude toward herself. A week after her first video and after seeing it, she says:

> ...It was exciting to see the video even though I remembered everything what I said... It would be nice to watch this video after ten years and see how I reacted... And how my life is then...

Discussion

Although the WDP was designed with both therapeutic and research aims in mind, the overall objective was to provide a space in which depressed women were able to talk about their depression in their own words. While there has been an increasing amount of description of depression from the lay perspective (Lewis ,1995; Tontti, 2000; Kangas, 1999, 2001), there is a paucity of qualitative research about practical psychiatric work, both evaluative and developmental, in this field (Isohanni, 1998) carried out by a treater.

On a therapeutic level, video recording presented an opportunity for both client and therapist to evaluate work that goes on in therapy sessions. It provided a therapeutic tool for future use. The therapeutic purpose was to help women to see and evaluate their current situations in terms of problems, life dilemmas, treatments they had experienced and ideas about their future. Here, the assumption was that when a group member watched herself being interviewed on a video monitor, it helped her to "see herself as others saw her," providing a mirroring effect. On this therapeutic level, the first author is an inside participant in the mental health field as a therapist of these patients. Through this "insider approach", the researcher belongs to the field by her occupation and is able to record her own impressions of being a part of the action (Maione & Chenail, 2001).

Video recording as a research tool provided a mechanism for feedback on experiences of depression "in members' own words." It also provided a temporal, visual embodied context in which a group member along with the group leader/therapist could chart her passage through her depression experience and WDP group processes.

In a real sense, the video interview was a visual narrative of the therapeutic session as well as visual data on embodied experiences of depression. It allowed a member to focus on a longstanding problem that, in her view, had led to the path of her depression. As we have seen, troubles with a partner, work or studies, with oneself or worries about family member(s) were viewed as key depression-generating problems. On the one hand, a respondent's telling of these problems becomes an enactment of memory, pain and emotions. On the other hand, these problems become embedded in a visual, healing narrative upon which a member reflects.

It becomes clear that the video was not only used to collect data on "depression initiating" problems: it was also used as a technique to reveal to members that depression is a complex phenomenon. It is "experiences which arise in conjunction with one's embodied efforts to meet socially constructed standards defining a good woman" (Stoppard, 2000: 108). Thus, troubles with a partner, work or studies, with oneself or worries about family member/s, while viewed as key problems by members, were not the only source of their depression. Rather, their depression is the outcome of processes of shared interactions between one's physical embodiment and one's constructed experiences. In this sense, the video becomes one important way for members to visualise this interaction and to build upon their own healing narratives. Researchers have argued that without visual identity there is no presence, and that this means no social support networks and no community (Ainley, 1995, cited in Holliday, 2000: 122). Whether or not the women of the WDP found a strong sense of community through video interviews, they could at least come to a sense of their own visual identity which gave them potential for community participation. As Denzin (1995: 1) has said:

> ...the postmodern is a visual cinematic age; it knows itself in part through the reflections that flow from the camera's eye. The voyeur is the iconic postmodern self. Adrift in a sea of symbols, we find ourselves voyeurs, all products of cinematic gaze.

While depressed women in this study are a part of this cinematic gaze, through video interviews they have at least experienced their own visual identity, which is a product of the problems which form in their depressive experiences. Hopefully, the findings in this paper have mapped out areas for further exploration about using video interviews as both a research and therapeutic tool with depressed women.

Bibliography

Angus, L., and D. Rennie. "Envisioning the Representational World: The Client's Experience of Metaphoric Expression in Psychotherapy." *Psychotherapy*, 26 no. 3 (1989): 372–379.

Ball, M. S., and G. W. H. Smith. *Analyzing Visual Data.* Newbury Park, CA: Sage. 1992.

Bauer, M. W., and G. Gaskill. *Qualitative Researching with Text, Image and Sound: A Practical Handbook.* London, England: Sage, 2000.

Bhui, K., and D. Olajide. *Health Service Provision for a Multicultural Society.* London, England: W. B. Sauders, 1999.

Biggs, S. J. "Introduction." in P. W. Dowrick and S. J. Biggs, *Using Video: Psychological and Social Applications*, 91–93. New York, NY: John Wiley and Sons, 1983.

Bodker, S. "Applying Activity Theory to Video Analysis: How to Make Sense of Video Data in Human-Computer Interaction." in B. A. Nandi, ed., *Context and Consciousness: Activity Theory and Human-Computer Interaction*, 147–174. Boston, MA: MIT Press, 1996.

Bottorff, J. L. "Using Videotaped Recordings in Qualitative Research." in J. M. Morse, ed., *Critical Issues in Qualitative Research Methods*, 244–261. Thousand Oaks, CA: Sage, 1994.

Denzin, N. *The Cinematic Society: The Voyeur's Gaze.* London, England: Sage, 1995.

Dowrick, P. W., and S. J. Biggs. *Using Video: Psychological and Social Applications.* New York, NY: John Wiley and Sons, 1983.

Emmison, M., and P. Smith. *Researching the Visual.* London, England: Sage Publications, 2000.

Falikov, C. J. "Culture, Society and Gender in Depression." *Journal of Family Therapy* 25 no. 4 (2003): 371–387.

Gilgun, J. F. "Definitions, Methodologies and Methods in Family Research." in J. F. Gilgun, K. Daly and G. Handel, eds., *Qualitative Methods in Family Research.* 22–39. Newbury Park, CA: Sage Publications, 1992.

Goodwin, C. "Recording Human Interaction in Natural Settings." *Pragmatics,* 3 no. 2 (1993): 181–209.

Harper, D. "Reimagining Visual Methods." in N. K. Denzin and Y. S. Lincoln, eds., *Handbook of Qualitative Research.* 2nd ed. 717–32. Thousand Oaks, CA: Sage, 2000.

Holliday, R. "We've Been Framed: Visualising Methodology." *The Sociological Review*, 48 no. 4 (2000): 503–521.

Hosford, R. E., and M. Mills. "Video in Social Skills Training." in P. W. Dowrick and S. J. Biggs., eds., *Using Video: Psychological and Social Applications.* 125–150. New York, NY: John Wiley and Sons, 1983.

Isohanni, M. "Tampereen yliopiston terveystieteen laitoksen arviointi. *Sosiaalilääketieteellinen Aikakauslehti.*" 35 (1998): 190.

Kangas, I. Maalikoiden masennuskertomukset ja-käsitykset. *Sosiaalilääketieteellinen Aikakauslehti* 36 (1999): 345–356.

Kangas, I. "Making Sense of Depression: Perceptions of Melancholia in Lay Narratives." *Health* 5 (2001): 76–92.

Laitinen, I. *Depression in/ by/for Women: Agency, Feminism and Self-help in Group.* Helsinki, Finland: University of Helsinki Press, 2008.

Laitinen, I., and E. Ettorre. "The Women and Depression Project: Feminist Action Research and Guided Self-Help Groups Emerging from the Finnish Women's Movement." *Women's Studies International Forum,* 27 (2004): 203–21.

—. "Diary Work with Depressed Women in Time-Limited, Professionally Guided Groups in the Finnish State-funded Health Service." *Journal of Poetry Therapy,* 20 no. 1 (2007): 1–18.

Laitinen, I., E. Ettorre and C. Sutton. "Empowering Depressed Women: Changes in 'Individual' and 'Social' Feelings in Guided Self-Help Groups in Finland." *European Journal of Psychotherapy and Counselling,* 8 no. 3 (2006): 305–20.

—. "Gaining Agency through Healthy Embodiment in Groups for Depressed Women." *European Journal of Psychotherapy and Counselling,* 9 no. 2 (2007): 1–19.

Lewis S. "A Search for Meaning: Making Sense of Depression." *Journal of Mental Health* 4 (1995): 369–382.

Loizos, P. "Video, Film, and Photographs as Research Documents." in M. W. Bauer and G. Gaskill, eds., *Qualitative Researching with Text, Image and Sound: A Practical Handbook.* 93–107. London, England: Sage, 2000.

Maione, P., and R. Chenail. "Qualitative Inquiry in Psychotherapy: Research on the Common Factors." in M. A. Hubble, B. L. Duncan and S. D. Miller, eds., *The Heart and Soul of Change: The Role of Common Factors in Psychotherapy.* pp. 57–88. Washington D.C.: American Psychological Association, 2001.

McRea, C. "Impact on Body-Image." in P. W. Dowrick and S. J. Biggs, eds., *Using Video: Psychological and Social Applications.* 95–103. New York, NY: John Wiley and Sons, 1983.

Nazroo, J. *Ethnicity and Mental Health.* London, England: Policy Studies Institute, 1997.

Renne, C., P. W. Dowrick and G. Wasek. "Considerations of the Participant in Video Recording." in P. W. Dowrick and S. J. Biggs, eds., *Using Video: Psychological and Social Applications.* 23–32. New York, NY: John Wiley and Sons, 1983.

Rennie, D. "Storytelling in Psychotherapy: The Client's Subjective Experience." *Psychotherapy,* 31 no. 2 (1994): 234–243.

Stoppard, J. *Understanding Depression.* London, England: Routledge, 2000.

—. "Women's Bodies, Women's Lives and Depression: Towards a Reconciliation of Material and Discursive Accounts." in Jane M. Ussher, ed., *Body Talk: The Material and Discursive Regulation of Sexuality, Madness and Reproduction.* 10–33. London, England: Routledge, 1997.

Tontti, J. Masennuksen arkea. Selityksiä surusta ilman syytä. *Sosiaalipsykologisia tutkimuksia.* Helsinki, Finland: University of Helsinki, 2000.

Ulmer, G. *Teletheory: Grammatology in an Age of Video.* New York, NY: Routledge, 1989.

THE ROLE OF COMMUNITY-BASED GROUPS IN THE PREVENTION AND RECOVERY OF POSTNATAL DEPRESSION

SHARI READ AND DEBRA RICKWOOD

The aim of this research was to examine the role of group membership with regard to positive mental health outcomes for women with young children. Specifically, the research was designed to explore whether community-based groups provide aspects of prevention and health promotion in supporting otherwise isolated stay-at-home mums with young children. The groups included in the research were based on a model of operation which aims to increase social connectedness, provide peer support for parenting, increase well-being, reduce the risk of postnatal depression and other mental illness, increase self-esteem, and develop community. The research employed a questionnaire-based survey of three groups of women, those who participated in a community-based women's group, women who participated in one of a number of ACT playgroups, and stay-at-home mums who were not participating in a parenting-related community group at the time of the research. Analysis compared each of the research groups on measures of social connectedness, group belonging and support, resilience and postnatal depression. Results are discussed in terms of the value of community-based parenting groups in health promotion, prevention and recovery of postnatal depression.

Introduction

Previous research has identified the need for community programs targeting women with young children (Box, 2005). It has been suggested that women are more likely to experience mental health problems during the postpartum period than at any other time in their lives, and social isolation is common for mothers who choose to stay at home (NHMRC, 2000). Many health programs and studies have established and examined parenting groups facilitated by nursing or other health professionals;

however, there has been growing support for community-based parenting groups where parents are empowered to play an active role in the development and management of the group (Tomison & Wise, 1999; Prilleltensky & Nelson, 2000). Fostering a sense of community is thought to have important health benefits (Smith, Baugh-Littlejohns & Thompson, 2001), and community-based parenting groups have been found to improve parenting skills and self-esteem (Zeedyk, Werritty & Riach, 2003), and enhance social support networks (Prilleltensky & Nelson, 2000) and thus resilience.

Many women at home with young children feel profoundly isolated as they face the challenges of the parenting role and adjust to it. For women, the postnatal period is a time of particular vulnerability to mood disorders which carry significant risks, not only for the women concerned but also for their children and partners. The importance of infant attachment, early positive parenting and the family and social environment during the first three years of development is well documented (Milgrom, Martin & Negri, 1999). These foundations of a child's cognitive and emotional development can be jeopardised by maternal mental health problems such as postnatal depression.

Studies have consistently shown that between 10 and 20 percent of Australian women experience postnatal depression and a further 35 percent experience some form of distress or anxiety during the first year of their baby's life (Najman, Andersen, Bor, O'Callaghan, & Williams, 2000). Based on the high incidence of mental health problems in mothers, there is a need for interventions that target this high-risk group in an attempt to prevent or reduce the known risk factors.

This report provides preliminary findings of the evaluation of the Majura (MWG) and Brindabella (BWG) Women's Groups with respect to social inclusion, community development and mental health promotion. The MWG and BWG were established for mothers at home who are the primary carers of infants and young children in an attempt to decrease their vulnerability to mental health problems. The Groups aim to increase some of the protective factors for both mothers and children using a creative and economical approach enhancing community networks.

The project involved collection of data from women participating in the MWG and BWG. For comparison purposes, data were also collected from women participating in one of a number of ACT playgroups and also from stay-at-home mums who were not currently members of a parenting-related community group. By comparing data from the MWG/BWG to those from women who attend playgroups and women who are not members of a community group, the benefits unique to participation in the Majura or Brindabella Women's Groups may be uncovered.

The evaluation focused primarily on the sense of connectedness and belonging that the MWG/BWG may engender in their individual participants, and the potential positive effects on mental health and well-being of the women involved. The research is essentially quantitative, designed to measure changes in aspects of group participation and the associated psychological benefits to the individuals. There is also a qualitative aspect of the research designed to identify the elements and processes of the MWG/BWG that women find beneficial.

The overall aim of the evaluation research was to determine whether there was a change for the women in the MWG/BWG in terms of social connectedness, mental health, and parenting over the course of the program, and compared with both a matched group of women in the community participating in an alternate program and a group of women in the community not participating in such a program.

Methodology

The evaluation employed a mixed design. As well as the target groups, the MWG and BWG, the study included both a comparison group (playgroup mums) and a control group (stay-at-home mums who were not parenting/community group members).

The research was designed to explore the process and outcome measures revealing the benefits of group membership and involved collection of data from a sample of women who currently participate in:

- the Majura or Brindabella Women's Groups;
- a selection of ACT Playgroups (chosen to match the geographical areas where the women's groups meet);
- collection of data from women who were primarily stay-at-home mums and do not participate in either of the above community groups at the time of data collection.

Participants

Research participants were:
- thirty-two members of the MWG or BWG;
- forty-eight playgroup members; and
- nineteen mothers who did not currently participate in a parenting-related community group.

Measures

In evaluating the effectiveness of the MWG/BWG in providing social support to stay-at-home mothers, a primarily quantitative approach was taken, however, a number of open-ended questions were included to assess some aspects of quality:

Demographic measures included:

- The number of women who attend the Group and their parenting situation (e.g. number and ages of children, co-parenting/sole parenting status);
- The pattern of session attendance for members/attendees;
- Duration of involvement in the Group
- Relevant measures of socio-economic disadvantage (e.g. last completed education); and
- Open-ended questions regarding reasons for joining the group and perceived benefits.

Quantitative/outcome measures. The Sense of Belonging Scale, adapted from Glynn (1981), was used to measure belongingness to the group for Playgroup and Women's Group members. Higher scores represent a stronger sense of belonging to the group. The scale attained a high level of internal consistency in the current sample with a Cronbach alpha coefficient .93.

To assess the quality of group participation, an adaptation of the Organisational Trust Inventory (Cummings & Bromiley, 1996) was used. The scale has been widely used in organizational psychology research and attained an alpha of .94 with the current sample.

Social support was measured using the Interpersonal Support Evaluation List (ISEL) (Cohen & Hoberman, 1983). This instrument measures four sub-scales of social support, three of which were used in the current study—appraisal, belonging and tangible support. Consistent with previous research, the sub-scales showed good internal consistency in the current sample with Cronbach alphas of .71, .76 and .73, respectively.

A revised version of the Parenting Satisfaction Scale (Guidubaldi & Cleminshaw, 1994) was used to measure how mothers felt about themselves in this role. The scale was designed to measure attitudes towards parenting and attained an alpha coefficient of .63 in this sample.

The Rosenberg Self-Esteem Scale (Rosenberg, 1965) was adapted to assess women's self-esteem as a mother. High scores reflected high-self esteem as a mother and the alpha coefficient attained with this sample was .87.

To measure women's feelings of self-esteem in respect to them being grouped with other mothers, an adapted version of the Collective Self-Esteem Scale (Luhtanen & Crocker, 1992) was used. High scores on this scale reflect strong positive feelings about the role of motherhood. The Cronbach alpha coefficient attained in this sample was .74.

A Social Capital Scale (MacDonald, 2006) was used to measure women's perceived level of connection to their community. The scale was based on items used in a general social survey conducted by the Australian Bureau of Statistics in 2002 and 2006. High scores reflect a stronger sense of connection within the local community. The analysis of internal consistency revealed an alpha of .63.

The Edinburgh Postnatal Depression Scale (Cox, Holden & Sagovsky, 1987) was included to measure levels of postnatal depression. The scale is widely used and recognized as one of the primary tools for screening for postnatal depression. Scores range from 0 to 30, and in a primary health setting women with scores above 12 would be offered further assessment. Internal consistency analysis revealed an alpha of .84 in this sample.

The Connor-Davidson Resilience Scale (Connor & Davidson, 2003) was used to assess relative susceptibility to psychological disorder. High scores reflect a stronger level of resilience and the scale attained an internal consistency coefficient of .90 in this sample.

Procedure

All participants in the MWG/BWG and comparison group (Playgroup) were approached during session times and invited to participate in the research. Invitations to participate were also included in the newsletters of each of the respective groups. Questionnaire booklets were distributed in sessions and those members who chose to participate in the research completed the questionnaire in their own time.

Stay-at-home mums who were not members of a community group were recruited through informal networks and represent a convenience sample. A snow-balling technique was used to increase numbers in this sample. All participants received a replied-paid envelope to return the questionnaire to the researchers. Participation in the research was voluntary Ethics approval was obtained from the University of Canberra Committee for Ethics in Human Research.

All participants received a consent form to sign and return, a cover letter from the researchers explaining the nature of the research (participant information), and a list of community resources and phone numbers should they identify a need for further support.

Results

The MWG/BWG participants, Playgroup participants and control group were comparable on both age (ranging from under twenty-five to over forty) and number of children, with a range of one to six.

Of the MWG/BWG mums, 61.3 percent were full-time stay-at-home mums at the time of data collection, while 78.3 percent of Playgroup mums and 72.2 percent of the control group mums reported being in the same situation. The majority of mothers from both groups who reported working outside of the home were in paid employment for two to three days per week. While the difference in the percentage of women who were not full-time stay-at-home mums was not statistically significant (X^2 [3, N=97] = 2.203, $p < .531$), it is of note given that one of the principles underlying the MWG's model of operation is to be available to women in this situation.

Almost 13 percent (12.9 percent) of MWG/BWG mums reported being single parents, with only 2.1 percent of Playgroup mums and 5.6 percent of control group mums reporting this, suggesting that the MWG model of operation may be effective in this area.

The groups were also well matched with regard to education levels, with around 73 percent of MWG/BWG members having completed a tertiary degree, and around 63 percent and 56 percent of Playgroup and control group mums respectively having completed a university-level qualification.

It is important to note that 12.9 percent of the MWG/BWG participants also attended a playgroup. All of these women completed the questionnaire with reference to the Women's Group (either the MWG or BWG) that they attended.

There was no difference between the MWG/BWG and Playgroup members on length of attendance, with both groups having an average group membership length of one and a half years (range one week to six years). The frequency of attendance patterns was also similar between the two groups, with the majority of women attending their community group on a weekly basis.

Qualitative Findings

There were eight open-ended questions included in the questionnaire regarding women's experiences in their group (not included for the control group). Overall, it was found that women in the MWG/BWG and Playgroups were very happy with their group and commented on feeling connected to other adults as well as receiving support as a mother. Most women reported encouraging other mums to join a group similar to their own (if not the same group) and felt that groups of this nature deserve community and government support.

Outcome measures. The majority of women in both the MWG/BWG and Playgroup groups scored high on the Sense of Belonging Scale (Group Belonging), members of the MWG/BWG had a mean of 6.4 on a 7 point scale (with a range of 1.4 – 7).

Ratings on the Group Trust Inventory (Group Trust) were also quite high, with a mean rating of 6 for both groups. The MWG/BWG members had a range of 1.5 – 7 with slightly fewer women rating a perfect 7, representing complete trust in the group, compared to the Playgroup mums (10.3 percent compared to 19.1 percent).

The Interpersonal Social Support Evaluation List is interpreted over three subscales: Social support – appraisal; Social support – tangible; and Social support – belonging. Ratings on the appraisal and tangible social support subscales were similar between the three groups, however, MWG/BWG participants perceived a significantly higher level of social support in terms of *belonging* from their group, $t(76) = 2.2$, $p < .03$ when compared to the Playgroup mums.

There was also a significant difference between the MWG/BWG and Playgroup mums for ratings on the Parenting Satisfaction Scale (Satisfaction as a Mother), with Playgroup mums rating their level of satisfaction as a mother significantly higher than their counterparts in the MWG/BWG . The difference between the two groups arises primarily as a result of differences in responses to two of the scale items, which were less strongly endorsed in the MWG/BWG:

- *Sacrificing for my children is a part of motherhood;* and
- *My children are the number one priority in my life.*

Ratings on the Rosenberg Self-Esteem Scale and the Collective Self-Esteem Scale were similar for each of the three groups, as were scores on the Social Capital Scale.

Scores on the Edinburgh Postnatal Depression Scale (PND) were not significantly different between the groups; however, it is important to note that in each of the groups there were women who scored within the range for clinical concern (i.e. score >12). In the MWG/BWG, 20 percent of respondents had a score above 12 while 16.6 and 8.5 percent of respondents from the control group or a Playgroup respectively had a score that fell above this mark. While this difference is not statistically significant (X^2 [1, N=77] = 2.14, p <.144), it does suggest that women experiencing postnatal depression are finding their way to one of the Women's Groups for support.

There was no difference between the groups with regard to mean ratings on the Resilience measure.

Discussion

Based on the data collected from women participating in either the Majura or Brindabella Women's Group or a Playgroup, it appears that the groups are generally attracting women who are:

- Older than twenty-five years and in their mid-thirties;
- mothers of one or two children;
- well-educated with a tertiary level qualification;
- either full-time stay-at-home mums or in part-time employment; and
- co-parenting with a partner (i.e. not single mums).

Participants seem to continue their membership in either group for well over one year and usually attend weekly.

Overall, participants in the MWG or BWG and Playgroups report being very happy with the benefits of group membership. There seems to be a strong theme of women joining one of the groups on the basis of a recommendation from either a friend or their community health nurse, or because they are looking for social support (which they report finding).

The defining difference between the MWG/BWG and the Playgroups is the adult focus of the Women's Groups, particularly through their art projects. Whereas the Playgroup mums primarily reported the benefits of membership being communication and friendship, the MWG/BWG mums added creativity and inspiration to the list. There seems to be a strong sense of belonging to the group and high levels of trust within groups for the majority of the research participants. Furthermore, there are high levels of perceived social support in both groups.

The difference in scores on the Satisfaction as a Mother Scale may reflect the qualitative differences between the MWG/BWG and Playgroup's respective models of operation. MWG/BWG mums may feel less pressure to make sacrifices for their children and always put their children's needs first, suggesting that these groups might serve to encourage and facilitate women's own sense of well-being as an individual.

Levels of both individual and collective self-esteem were moderately high for all three groups, and MWG/BWG, Playgroup and control group participants reported perceiving good levels of social capital in their communities.

The PND scale revealed numbers of women experiencing postnatal depression in the overall sample that match expected levels reported in the general population (13 percent), however, the elevated numbers found among WG participants (20 percent compared to 8.5 percent amongst playgroup mums and 16.6 percent in the control group) suggests that women with PND are attracted to the Women's group. This places a responsibility on the MWG/BWG to ensure that their community is a safe and supportive environment for women vulnerable to mental illness. Having said this, based on the qualitative data collected from this sample, it appears that the women feel well supported and perceive direct mental health benefits from participation in their Women's Group. However, levels of resilience were no different to those found among Playgroup mums (being moderately high in both groups) so resilience-building may prove to be an area for further development if the MWG/BWG intend to continue their work in supporting women with mental health issues.

The good work of the MWG/BWG becomes clear when results on each of the measures is interpreted in context of the high level of postnatal depression among the members of these groups. Despite one in five of MWG/BWG mums revealing a level of postnatal depression that would warrant clinical concern, the groups were still rated highly on the measures of belonging and trust, social capital and social support. Furthermore, members had similarly high levels of individual and collective self-esteem and resilience as Playgroup mums, suggesting that not only are the MWG/BWG accessible to women with PND, they are providing valuable resources to these women to support recovery.

Acknowledgments

The authors would like to acknowledge contributions to the research from Sue Hoffman and the Majura and Brindabella Women's Group committee members and Steve Druitt from the ACT Health, Mental Health Policy Unit. This research was funded by the HealthPact Research Centre for Health Promotion and Wellbeing.

Bibliography

Box, N. *Evaluation of the First Year of the Brindabella Women's Group*. Bruce, ACT: University of Canberra, 2005.

Cohen, S., and H. Hoberman. "Positive Events and Social Supports as Buffers of Life Change Stress." *Journal of Applied Social Psychology*, 13 (1983): 99–125.

Connor, K., and J. Davidson. "Development of a New Resilience Scale: The Connor-Davidson Resilience Scale (CD-RISC)." *Depression and Anxiety*, 18 (2003): 76–82.

Cox, J., J. Holden and R. Sagovsky. "Detection of Postnatal Depression: Development of the 10-item Edinburgh Postnatal Depression Scale." *British Journal of Psychiatry*, 150 (1987): 782–86.

Cummings, L., and P. Bromiley. "The Organizational Trust Inventory (OTI): Development and Validation." In R. Krammer and T. Tyler, eds., *Trust in Organizations*. Newbury Park, CA: Sage, 1996.

Glynn, T. "Psychological Sense of Community: Measurement and Application." *Human Relations*, 34 (1981): 780–818.

Guidubaldi, J., and H. Cleminshaw. *Parenting Satisfaction Scale*. San Antonio, TX: PsychCorp, 1994.

Luhtanen, R., and J. Crocker. "A Collective Self-Esteem Scale: Self-Evaluation of One's Social Identity." *Personality & Social Psychology Bulletin*, 18 (1992): 302–18.

Macdonald, E. *Bushfire Recovery Survey*. Based on questions from General Social Survey (2002, 2006) with permission of Australian Bureau of Statistics. 2006.

Milgrom, J., P. R. Martin and L. Negri. *Treating Postnatal Depression: A Psychological Approach for Health Care Practitioners*. Chichester, England: Wiley & Sons, 1999.

Najman, J., M. Andersen, W. Bor, M. O'Callaghan and G. Williams. "Postnatal Depression—Myth and Reality: Maternal Depression Before and After the Birth of a Child." *Social Psychiatry and Psychiatric Epidemiology*, 35 no. 1 (2000): 19–27.

National Health and Medical Research Council (NHMRC). *Postnatal Depression: Not Just the Baby Blues*. Canberra, Commonwealth of Australia: NHMRC, 2000.

Prilleltensky, I., and G. Nelson. "Promoting Child and Family Wellness: Priorities for Psychological and Social Interventions." *Journal of Community and Applied Social Psychology*, 10 (2000): 85–105.

Rosenberg, M. *Society and the Adolescent Self-Image*. Princeton, NJ: Princeton University Press, 1965.

Smith, N., L. Baugh-Littlejohns and D. Thompson. "Shaking Out the Cobwebs: Insights into Community Capacity and its Relation to Health Outcomes." *Community Development Journal,* 36 no. 1 (2001): 30–41.

Tomison, A., and S. Wise. Community-Based Approaches in Preventing Child Maltreatment. *National Child Protection Clearinghouse— Australian Institute of Family Studies,* 11 (Autumn 1999): 1–17.

Zeedyk, S., I. Werritty and C. Riach. "The PALS Parenting Support Programme: Lessons Learned from the Evaluation Process and Outcomes." *Children & Society,* 16 (2003): 318–33.

OVERCOMING DEPRESSION AND FEMALE LEARNED HELPLESSNESS THROUGH HYPNOTHERAPY

TRACIE O'KEEFE

This is a discursive paper illustrated by four women's cases where they were able to overcome their sense of depression by learning a greater sense of self-efficacy during hypnotherapy. In Australia, as in every other country in the world, girls and women are of less social, work, economic, religious and political importance than males. Women learn from a very early age not only to acquiesce to perceived male superiority, but also to generally not pursue power over their own lives. Because Australia comprises such a wide mix of people of varying ethnic derivations, women's liberation is at times is years behind that of North America and Europe.

Many women in Australia have been raised in family structures that value males over females. This can profoundly undermine girls' and women's sense of ego, self-differentiation and efficacy. Such learned helplessness is supported by a society where few women are industry, religious or political leaders, not through choice but exclusion.

In this paper I look at four women who were helped in relation to a sense of depression through hypnotherapeutic intervention and personality alteration. Hypnotherapy has proved to be an accelerated form of personality re-invention and supplementation that can help women find their voices and strengths in a very short period of time. As a goal-focused therapy, hypnotherapy has shown itself to be one of the quickest forms of personality change methods without resulting to what are often over-prescribed medications that frequently oppress women, rather than support them.

Introduction

When a person is depressed they can have a sense of unhappiness, helplessness, despair, sullenness, impending doom, tiredness, exhaustion, lack of energy and lack of self-efficacy. They are unable to focus on the positive aspects of life and become obsessed with the negative aspects of their existence. Along with those psychological difficulties, a physical malaise also takes over the body and people have a sense of not being in the best of health, wellbeing or spirits (Beck, 1973).

There are two kinds of basic depression identified in medicine and psychology. The first is endogenous depression that is the result of illness or profound chemical changes in the body due to an upset of homeostasis, which is the balancing of the body's systems, causing secondary psychological effects. The second kind of depression is called exogenous or reactive depression, which is the result of a person experiencing primarily psychological reactions to a situation which then activates physical symptoms (Sperry, 1994).

In some cases people are diagnosed as manic depressives in that they continually swing from an extreme of heightened manic happiness to a very low state of morbid depression (Fuller, Torrey & Knable, 2002). The allopathic medical model considers this a mental illness and generally medicates in the first instance, very rarely offering psychological help.

Depression is also graded as minor or major in accordance with its severity, debilitating effects and length of duration. In grading and looking at depressive behaviors, a clinician needs to also remember cultural influences and ideations that may have a major effect on how they see a patient and how the patient sees themselves and their own experiences. Breggin (1993) observed that depression is recorded more in cultures where there is great profit from treating the concept of depressive illnesses, particularly through hospitalisation, electric convulsive therapy (ECT), and psychopharmacology.

Laing (1985) talked about how, after many years of practice, he came to believe that the institution of medicine often becomes just that—an institution. His work was largely responsible for the decommissioning of many mental health hospitals internationally in that he saw medicine as often being devoid of human understanding. He was particularly horrified by the way women were treated by the medical profession when they had psychological difficulties, seeing standard prescriptions as not being the way forward for women experiencing psychological and emotional difficulties.

Pope (2001) talked about how what is often forgotten in our culture, in the English-speaking world, is that depression is part of the menstrual cycle, which has a function. Women experience many kinds of depressive states at differing times of their lives, including times when they are premenstrual, ovulating, menopausal, post-partum, dealing with empty nest syndrome, ageing or during illness. Natural depressive states for women are constantly being misdiagnosed as illness and not natural functions. Instead of telling women to find space to be alone to rest and recover, physicians are all too often unnecessarily administering drugs. Our society, it seems, considers lack of productivity the real illness in women that it seeks to fix with pharmacology and sometimes electric shock treatment in order to create corporate profit.

Many women present themselves to their doctors complaining of depression are primarily offered poor and unproven drug therapy. Moore (1998), a senior fellow in health policy at George Washington University Medical Centre, writes:

> Nearly every one of the most popular prescription drugs has potential side effects, yet doctors seldom discuss them for fear that patients will be too frightened to take their medicine. For example, Motrin, Advil, and Aleve may cause life-threatening perforated ulcers; Prozac is linked to 242 different adverse effects; Xanax can be highly addictive. Tranquilisers, sleep aids, painkillers reduce blood pressure—all have documented risks. (Publisher's Note)

Jensvold, Halbreich and Hamilton said:

> Until recently, women were excluded as research subjects from much pharmacological research, including the early phases of drug testing and numbers of prominent large studies, as well as many smaller studies. Also commonly, when women have been included in drug research, data have not been analysed with regard to sex and have not been reported in a manner that allows such analyses to be performed. Factors unique to women have often been used as justification for excluding women from drug research. (1996: 4)

This means many of the medications currently being prescribed to women for depression have not been tested on women. There is no knowledge of how those medications affect the hormonal cycles of women, or how the hormonal cycles affect the medications' reactions on the body.

Since Australia was a British colony, much of European-type immigrant Australian culture over the past two hundred years has been based on Judeo-Christian theology. Within the past thirty years a large influx of Asian and Muslim communities has been added, but mainly in the cities. There are also the native Aboriginal cultures, a smaller part of the population, who do use the services of Western allopathic medicine but also rely on traditional community support and medicine (Census of

Population and Housing, 2001).

In the Christian and Judaic traditions, Adam and Eve were not made equal: she was made as a companion and servant for him, as an afterthought. Eve got Adam thrown out of the Garden of Eden due to her initiating the act of original sin. She is still seen as the temptress to be resisted and excluded from power in the churches and the temple. In these religions, people's sexual and political power is purposely kept out of the hands of women by men (Hendrickson, 2000).

In the *Encyclopedia of Feminism*, Tuttle writes: "Traditionally Jewish women have been subordinate to men and forced to lead restricted lives" (1986: 156). She goes on to talk about how many Jewish women have been liberated in the twentieth century. In truth, however, in Jewish communities men are still the ones who hold the major power financially and in employment.

Chang tells us about three generations of women brought up in China:

> The story of his wife, my great-grandmother, was typical of millions of Chinese women of her time. She came from a family of tanners called Wu. Because her family was not an intellectual one and did not hold any official post, and because she was a girl, she was not given a name at all. (1993: 29)

Mosteshar, who was born in Iran and educated in Britain, and then returned to Iran, describes the choices of oppressed Muslim women in Iran and many other countries:

> Then they were shown various methods of contraception and advised to use them "until you are sure that the man you are married to will be the man you want to stay with." Few of these girls had ever spoken a dozen words to the boys who were downstairs preparing to turn them into women. Most of the brides told me that their grooms had been chosen by their parents or that they were their cousins. (1995: 245)

Roddick, the world-famous entrepreneur who started her own chain of cosmetic stores, The Body Shop, wrote:

> Is it far harder for a woman to be an entrepreneur? Certainly the enterprise culture is full of contradictions for women. On the one hand you are encouraged to get out there and conduct your own destiny, but on the other hand there is the very strong moral authority of home and hearth—the idea that we should be with our kids. It is still far easier for any women to go to the bank and secure a loan for a new kitchen or fitted wardrobes than one for starting a business. There is still the prevailing notion that women don't have the necessary business skills. (2000: 41)

There are still far fewer women in Parliament in Australia percentage-wise than many other countries, even though it has been 120 years since the formation of the Women's Suffragette League that was formed to get women the vote (NSW Parliament, March 2006).

In a lot of ways Australia is many years behind many English-speaking countries, such as Britain and North America and even some parts of Europe concerning the way in which women are not integrated into controlling society and their own lives. Australia is still very much a masculine-oriented culture, with very few women at the top of industry or politics. Many women were and are still being brought up with little concept that they are able to do and be anything they want in life, instead being seen as second-class citizens. Many first-, second- and third-generation Australians come from cultures where women still have much less value or importance and power than men:

> The inferior social and economic position of women, gender bias in the law, lack of access to legal services and lack of concerted government action continue to underpin women's legal inequality in Australia. Those suffering special disadvantage include Aboriginal and Torres Strait Islander women, women of non-English speaking background, women living in rural and remote areas, older women, women with a disability and women who are multiply disadvantaged. (National Women's Justice Coalition, 1997: para. 1)

There are also groups of people whom I wish to mention in my discussion who damage the central egos of many female children and women. They can include women themselves, who are part of certain groups of separatist feminists, as well as female religious fantasists. They are elite idealists who preach to women about what they should and should not be and are extremely judgmental.

Women with overbearing religious or philosophical ideations can foist doctrine so oppressively upon their daughters that they are left with feelings of insecurity and inadequacy, in that the daughters can never live up to the mothers' standards. They are women who sometimes teach their daughters to give up their own power to their husbands out of religious duty in a male-dominated religion. These children become women, who become professional victims with a sense of powerlessness about being able to create their own life courses, happiness and wellbeing.

Gauld (1995) describes how hypnosis in varying forms has been used for thousands of years in the healing process of all human beings, from the Egyptians to modern times. Crasilneck and Hall (1985) write about how many different kinds of practitioners practise hypnosis including hypnotherapists, psychotherapists, counsellors, psychiatrists, anaesthesiologists, oncologists, dentists, social workers, nurses and sometimes educators. Erickson (Rossi, 1989) the twentieth century's premiere medical hypnotist, believed that in treating depression with hypnotic techniques the practitioner generally needs to have had training in the psychological and maybe physiological disciplines as well as hypnosis.

The use of hypnotherapy in the treatment of depression has been greatly explored by the psychologist and hypnotherapist Yapko (1992). He contests the validity of many psychopharmacological studies and their choice as a primary treatment in many cases of depression. He also talks about how there has been great fear around the use of hypnosis and ameliorating depressive states that he sees as being unfounded. His work clearly shows that the use of hypnosis can accelerate self-evolution, psychodynamic and cognitive therapy through brief hypnotic therapy.

The use of hypnotic techniques and considerations in treating women needs at times to be different than those used with men (Hornyak, 2000). Women's bodies are different from men's, and their life issues and illnesses are often different from those of men. While some hypnotic techniques can be used with men and women alike, some hypnotic therapies need to be specifically designed for women.

Aim

In this paper I will look at four cases of women who have improved and moved away from overly depressive states through the use of modern eclectic hypnotherapy, which is a combination of hypnosis and psychotherapy. All cases experienced a combination of endogenous and exogenous depression. In reporting and reviewing these cases I seek to show that such women can seek help from hypnotherapy—that is, other than a psychopharmacologically based remedy.

Results

Case 1: Sharon. Sharon telephoned me on the recommendation of her friend who had seen an article about me in a newspaper. Initially the friend telephoned me because she was concerned about how depressed Sharon had become since her friend had last visited Australia.

When she telephoned me herself, Sharon told me she was of Middle Eastern descent, her family were strict Muslims and she beseeched me that her husband must not know about her treatment. Since she was unused to the centre of Sydney, the friend dropped her off at the clinic and picked her up afterwards.

It was easy to see the extent of her involvement in her religious system, because Sharon wore a head scarf which covered all of her face, with only her eyes showing when she was in public. At age twenty-three she had already had four children, but all of them, she explained, are girls: she was depressed because her husband was not happy without a son.

The last birth had been nine months before. She was still breast feeding, and her husband was angry because she had not become pregnant again, so she could try for a son. It was quite easy to see from her description of her life, body language and her mood of deep solemnity that she was suffering from both post-natal and reactive depression. She was also overwhelmed by her isolated domestic life. If it were not for her friend, she would not have had the money to come for treatment.

During four sessions of hypnotherapy and teaching her self-hypnosis, she was able to reorganise her daily schedule, sharing the childcare with a cousin, visiting a family planning clinic for oral contraception (without her husband knowing), and joining a women-only gym. Her self-esteem strengthened and Sharon enlisted the help of her mother-in-law to persuade her husband to give her a few years before they tried for another baby.

The hypnotherapy was expediently useful in helping her take back control of her life and the self-hypnosis she was taught was something she could do every day in the privacy of her own home, without anyone else knowing that she had ever had help.

As Sharon took more control of her life she became fitter, more confident, and happier and the post-natal depression lifted. The friend eventually went back to the Middle East, but by that time Sharon had built a new network of helpers and she felt she was better able to cope with her life.

Case 2: Larna. Aged thirty-five, Larna had been involved with drugs since she was thirteen, taking amphetamines, ecstasy and smoking marijuana on a daily basis. She was a single working mother with a son of four, making her living in the sex industry in a brothel.

In recounting her history to me, Larna had talked about how she had always felt she was intellectually inferior and did not have the mental abilities to succeed in life. Due to her involvement with drugs at school, she had become estranged from mainstream education and gravitated towards other out-of-control drug abusers during the whole of her adult life.

The women in her family had not become ambitious professionals; they were mothers who simply worked to survive, bringing in additional income to the males' role as primary breadwinner. Added to this was the fact that the father of her child was articulate with deep religious convictions and not involved with her lifestyle in any way. When she saw him to give access to the child she constantly felt intimidated by him.

What was plain to me at the first interview was that she had very low self-esteem, poor self-image and a lack of positive self-belief. What immediately contrasted to that observation was that she had a good command of the English language, used quite complex sentence construction and was very articulate in her use of adjectives. The disparity indicated that she was in fact a very intelligent woman who was not aware of her own intellectual abilities and that no one from her background had ever emphasised to her how intellectually capable she probably was.

She sought therapy because she was depressed about her circumstances and wished to stop using drugs, get an education and live a different way of life. Over several hypnotherapy sessions, and the work she was set to do at home, she was able to become free of drugs, and stopped smoking. She learned to future-pace her own success, change her belief system and plan how she was going to start a degree programme to take her towards the profession in which she wanted to work. In saying this, I make no judgement on the sex industry: I see many clients who work in this area. As opposed to being depressed, Larna learnt to be involved in creating her own reality, cut herself some slack, and realise that she was much more capable than she had previously believed during her life.

Case 3: Diane. This patient was a thirty-five-year-old long-term psychiatric patient with a twenty-year history of admittance and discharge from mental hospitals for bouts of bi-polar II disorder. She had had more than eighty electric shock treatments (ECT). At the time of consultation Diane was in a depressive stage, on Lithium Carbonate and trying to progressively come off the tranquilisers that she had been taking for eighteen months. She also had a history of complex multiple drug abuse, usually with partners who were also drug abusers.

Previously to attending my clinic she had been seeing the same psychiatrist once a week for several years when she was not hospitalised. The psychiatrist was currently on a six-month sabbatical and she had not been offered an alternative. Diane sought help with her depression because she was living alone and trying to get over the break-up with her boyfriend, who had been a fellow psychiatric patient in a hospital and had been violent towards her.

Certain things struck me about this patient at the outset. Firstly, she was an absolutely compliant person who seemed to expect people to tell her what to do, including her family, the psychiatrist, and her ex-boyfriend. Secondly, she seemed very comfortable in the roles of daughter, victim, mentally ill member of the family, patient, and her ex-boyfriend's ex-girlfriend. Thirdly, she had only ever worked a couple of years up until she was twenty, after which her family had supplied her with a stipendiary from their large business interests but they had little contact with her. During hypnotherapy Diane was asked to construct a new kind of image of herself that was different from any she had ever had before. Through interactive psychotherapy and hypnotic suggestion, she was taught to be the kind of independent person that she had never associated with herself before.

Since she was very afraid of people thinking she was weird and an outcast, I insisted that she became much weirder and told her that I totally objected to her becoming normal in any way whatsoever (paradoxical intention). This was very shocking to her at first and then we designed a way of hypnotic dreaming for her to use at home for her unconscious mind to come up with new ways of becoming out of the ordinary.

I saw Diane for five hypnotherapy sessions, after which she was using daily self-hypnosis, had a belief in her own efficacy, had devised a regular daily schedule so that she could exercise, shop for fresh food, study and do some volunteer work at a local charity. One of the most useful things she said she acquired in therapy was an ability to define the boundaries in her relationships so that she let people into her world on her own terms. Her depression lifted, and for the first time in her life she found that she was quite comfortable being an individual pursuing her own interests.

Case 4: Martha. Martha presented with two main complaints which had led her to become very depressed and to consider suicide, even though as a devout Catholic she believed it was a sin. She had just had a bilateral mastectomy due to breast cancer; at the time she had been undergoing chemotherapy and radiotherapy. She had also suffered from long-term Irritable Bowel Syndrome (IBS), with alternate constipation and loose motions and was struggling to even keep food down after meals. All this, plus the fact that her niece was coping very well with her own bilateral mastectomy, made her feel she was a loser and had lost all her attractiveness to her husband.

Martha also told me that she had a very caring husband and three teenage sons who were doing the best they could to help her through her cancer treatment. Although she loved her niece, she felt overwhelmed by the fact that the niece seemed to be sailing though her treatment and remaining cheerful.

Initially I told Martha I could not help her because I was not qualified enough to do the job she had asked of me. Annoyed that she had travelled two hours to see me, she demanded I explain because I had said on the telephone that I did help people in her situation. I told her that I believed she had already given up on herself and what she was seeking was a magician—and I was not a magician. I could, however, teach her to be a magician herself, but only if she was prepared to treat herself with the things that I taught her.

Intrigued, she decided that she had nothing to lose and agreed to learn self-hypnosis and use it four times a day. I also got her to promise on the Bible that she would keep her word. We then started hypnotherapy to change her eating patterns, types of food consumed and reprioritise her daily schedule so that her sons and husband would be looking after themselves over the next six months.

She was taught psychoneuroimmunology to help combat the cancer, the ability to change her mental state, the differentiation of herself as a person apart from her family, and she was asked to teach those things to her niece. After a few hypnotherapy sessions Martha became more philosophical and decided to take one day at time and get as much out of that day as she was able to while taking care of herself first.

I saw her for six sessions and the depression quickly lifted as she learned how to control her eating and bowel movements. She also made plans to have breast reconstruction, but cancelled the surgery because her husband pleaded with her not to go through with the operation. Her self-esteem increased and she learnt the cancer had been a great physical blow to her, but if she took her time, she was able to cope and continually try to get better. What was new to her was that she began to see herself as a separate person, an individual and not just an appendage to her family, which was what she had been raised to think she should become.

Discussion

Each of these four cases were women who sought hypnotherapy from a private clinical hypnotherapist (me) to alleviate depression and become motivated toward resolutions. They all paid for their own treatments, bar one (who was funded by her friend); no one was funded by government heath funds. Some, however, did get partial rebates back from their private medical insurance companies. During treatment it became clear that they all suffered from low self-esteem and a lack of self-efficacy in their abilities to move beyond a depressive state. What became clear as well is that as women they did not believe they were capable enough to cope with whatever came their way. Either they had not learnt significant coping mechanisms in the first place for self-integrity; or the vagaries of life had led them to a place of dependency on the patriarchal all-powerful medical system; or they had been ill and felt that their self-reliant resources were depleted.

Three of the four patients reported that they had been prescribed antidepressants by their GPs but not gained any relief from them. The GPs had consulted with those patients for around five minutes each. None of those GPs referred the patients for any form of counselling or arranged any kind of follow-up with regard to the effects of the antidepressants. The one patient who had been previously identified as long-term bi-polar II seemed not to be supervised by anyone at the time. Breggin (1992) criticised at length the culture of allopathic medicine—GPs and psychiatrists prescribing unsubstantiated antidepressants at the drop of a hat without even finding out what was bothering the patient.

One of the major problems with the way allopathic Western medicine sees depression is that it always sees it as an illness. In trying to fix this pathology it administers chemical cocktails to change the body's levels of serotonin without dealing with the cause of the depression. This is rather like hitting the foot with a hammer to make it fit the larger shoe.

Australian women within the medical system who defy the patriarchal rule books are cited as upstarts and proletarians. Kerryn Phelps, the first female doctor to be the president of the Australian Medical Association, had to employ lawyers to defend her against defamation when the press over-profiled her because of her lesbian relationship (Mitchell, 2002).

Women's way through and out of depressive states needs to be different; they need different strategies than men by nature of their unique social positions and their long history of social oppression. This is the kind of oppression that has often been shared by gay, lesbian, bisexual, trans and intersex (GLBTI) cultures or people of ethnic derivation (Paglia, 1994). Just as Paglia demands that GLBTI people need to take charge of their own future, so do therapists dealing with women and depression need to charge their patients with responsibility for their own recovery.

Many Australian and international women have been made to feel subservient to the men in their families and have lowered career, social, personal, and economic expectations. The mental health system in Australia also has not yet grasped the concept of helping a client heal herself; doctors are still revered as omnipotent. So when medics tell women they have an illness called "depression" and they should take medication, that is what the client does, joining in what is often a folie à deux.

Women today in Australia still live mainly in a patriarchal culture and are taught a degree of helplessness and dependency from an early age. They perceive themselves as done to rather than doers. They are further disempowered when, experiencing natural depression, they are told that they have some kind of dreadful illness which can only be cured by drugs. This is often further exacerbated when even female medics join in the deception and prescribe unnecessary medical treatments when what is needed is caring and talking, not unproven pharmacological prescriptions.

It would be better to see being in a depressive state as a gift in that the mind and/or body is seeking to draw attention to a particular problem or situation. As human beings we are meant to experience sadness as it is part of the whole repertoire of experiences like happiness, anger, delight, jealousy or fear. It only becomes pathology in Western medicine because there are trillions of dollars to be made out of it by drug companies.

The four women in this study were required to change their exercise schedules, eating habits, prioritising and organisation of their lives. In treating depression, or, as it used to be known "melancholia", there is a need to consider all aspects of the person, including physical, mental, spiritual, and social. What is also important, and can be found out quickly through hypnotic regression, is the onset and possible causes of the melancholia:

- What purpose does it serve?
- To what does the person need to pay attention?
- What needs changing?
- What does the person need to do to move to the normal state of bodily homeostasis, which is happiness?
- How can the person once again, or even sometimes for the first time, lead a fulfilling life?

All four patients were predisposed to the idea that they could get help from hypnotherapeutic treatment and that help could be effective. With each of the patients I spent time in the first session suggesting expectation for change to them. They were also told that change at times could be dramatic and they were asked if they were ready for those kinds of changes to happen in their lives. This is what Erickson (Rossi, 1989) called a double bind. First the client was told that there would be change (expectation of change); then they were told that change may be dramatic (compounding the first suggestion); and then they were asked for assurances that they would be prepared for that kind of change when it came (double bind).

Patients were also made aware that they would have tasking (homework) that needed to done between sessions and that part of the therapy needed to be completed. My experience over the years has been that patients who task well always stand a better chance of therapy being effective and fast. This also makes therapy interactive and commits clients to being largely responsible for their own recovery, improving their egos, self-esteem and self-efficacy.

Repetitive homework with self-hypnosis on a daily basis is also a form of cognitive behaviour therapy in that it installs new behaviour programmes and cognitions through repetition. Depressed people need to break out of old ways of thinking and move onto new, more constructive automatic mindsets. What was of note from these four cases was that the women did not have a sense of their own personal power. These women did not experience an ego state that was sufficiently developed to support a belief that they could create what they wanted. Each woman had low self-esteem and lack of self-efficacy due to the way they were raised. They were not taught that they could not only meet life on their own terms but also create life on their own terms.

The hypnotherapy helped the four women in this study to experience and create fast cognitive, behavioural and experiential change. They learnt to change their moods and personal experiences at will, take charge of their lives and to be able cope with life regardless of what happens. In short, the four women matured into the kind of adult personalities that are self-dependent and self-servicing.

It is important to note that no matter how depressed a patient is, if they are motivated towards change, the placebo effect generally kicks in and magnifies any change, so the placebo effect becomes compounded. Some women, however, get caught up in vicious circles of depressive states, lack of ability to work and economic and social decline.

Feeling depressed arises from a sometimes simple or sometimes complex set of circumstances, psychological ideations and/or physical concomitants that are always different for every individual. No two patients are ever alike even though they can experience similar physical aspects or psychological themes. For women there are issues in therapy that are generally different from those of men, such as child-raising, access to education and economics, and legal rights. All of these issues in a woman's life contribute towards feelings of self-worth, ability to believe in herself, and ability to overcome life issues, and recover from depressive states and illness.

Women have special needs in therapy for depression because they carry with them their social history of oppression. Germaine Greer was born in Melbourne in 1939, went to England and published her famous book *The Female Eunuch* in the early 1970s which dealt with the call for women to further emancipate themselves from what is essentially a male-dominated world culture. She wrote:

> This book is part of the second feminist wave. The old suffragettes, who served their prison terms and lived on through the years of gradual admission of women into professions which they declined to follow, into parliamentary freedoms which they declined to exercise, into academies which they used more and more as shops where they could take out degrees while waiting to get married, have seen their spirit revive in younger women with a new and vital cast. (1973: 11)

Greer was right in some ways, in that many middle-class women do waste their opportunities for independence to differentiate themselves as individuals rather being a male appendage. However, Australia today is such a mixture of cultures and many of the women are from cultures where religion and social order dictate that women's needs are secondary to men's. Those women, of whatever class or derivation, have not been brought up with the belief that they can do and achieve anything they want. Part of their indoctrination has also been that they often see the medical establishment as the answer to all their ills and are easily led into the illusion that a pill can fix their woes during depression, but it seldom does.

The nature of women is that they are generally seen as the carers in our societies and that they do tend to operate on a micro-social level as opposed to a global macro level as men do. Men derive much of their power bases through associations and mutual support known as the "boys club". Knight (1983) in describing the Freemasons, taps into the very mechanism that gives men their power through politics, religion, brotherhoods and lifelong associations. Women, because they are often tethered to their families, do not have such strong support mechanisms and are left with a sense that they are without great self-power.

This idea becomes very clear when we look at women like Nicola Horlick (1997) an English woman who has been one of the leading directors of British pension funds, earning millions of pounds a year and also having several children at the same time. Horlick put her success down to the fact that she had attended a boys' school as a small child and, unlike many of her peers, grew up with the idea that she could achieve anything her male counterparts did. Even when dealing with a child who was diagnosed with leukaemia, she simply says that she took everything in her stride.

Need, however, is the mother of invention and women do have an inbuilt natural aptitude to regenerate themselves. The singer Marianne Faithfull (Hodkinson, 1991) tells us how after international fame in the 1960s she developed a heroin dependency, lost everything and lived on the streets of London's Soho during the 1970s. In the 1980s she totally reinvented herself again, shooting back to international acclaim for her work. Debbie Harry (Metz, 2002), who fronted the rock band Blondie, was the one of the famous American female rock singers of the 1970s who broke through to international fame, but gave everything up to care for her boyfriend who had a life-threatening disease for several years. As he recovered she had to build her career again virtually from the bottom upwards, and it took her twenty years to establish herself as a music legend.

Through the emergence of monotheism—the idea of one all-powerful male god, from around 2000 years ago—women lost their sense of power which was further decimated by the industrial revolution and the separation of women from nature. The reintroduction of matriarchy and pagan principles of the "mother the giver of life" (Straffon, 1997) and political liberation means that women are slowly regaining their personal power in some areas of the world. For many women, however, even in the depths of the most sophisticated societies, they are still bonded to the role of subservient second-class citizens. To overcome a depressive state a person needs a sense of personal power; and part of the redress for the four women in this study was that they left therapy with a sense that they were the ones in control of their own lives.

Perhaps Western allopathic medicine models can learn from the Aborigines of Australia about Wuriupranili (Wikipedia), a solar goddess who carries a torch that is the sun. In the ocean to the West, she douses the torch in water and uses the glowing embers to find her way beneath the earth back to the East again. The colours of dawn and dusk come from the ochre body paints she wears.

General practitioners and psychiatrists are generally the frontline for many patients who present themselves as suffering from depression or are in what is perceived as a depressed state. Those doctors fail in nearly all cases to distinguish between exogenous and endogenous depression but use a "sticking plaster" approach of prescribing dubiously tested antidepressant drugs to alleviate and remedy depression.

Those doctors adopt this approach for several reasons. They hope that for some patients the depressive state is transient and that it will pass shortly; and by giving the patient what they believe to be a cure, it will help the patient wait for change. Doctors also prescribe those medications in the hope that the very act of prescribing something will act as a psychological catalyst to commence a healing state in the patient. Such medications are also prescribed as a sugar pill depending on the placebo effect of the patients believing in the medication. Some doctors actually do believe in the efficacy of antidepressants.

Doctors also often prescribe such medications because they fear the consequences should they not prescribe those pills. Their medical associations give them strict guidelines to prescribe such medications and should the doctors stray from those guidelines they run the risk of being in breach of their insurance policies.

We can see from these four cases that women suffering from what they believed was depression were actually often dealing with life issues. Whether those issues arose as psychological reactions to circumstances or due to physical depletion of the body's wellness is immaterial. Each person suffering from depressive states was able to benefit from interpersonal reactions with me, the therapist trained to guide people through those states by hypnotherapeutic treatment.

Critique

This study only deals with four women who have presented themselves to a private health clinic for help with their self-identified states of depression. It does not deal with extremely economically disadvantaged women who are unable to afford the services of a private hypnotherapist.

The four cases reviewed were also women who were motivated towards change but felt they were unable to make it happen without help. This study does not deal with depressive women who are unmotivated towards change who have become chronically morbid, may be in the depths of mental illness or be of a paranoid or schizoid nature.

Conclusion

The four women in this study suffered from a self-identified state of depression and were successfully helped though hypnotherapeutic intervention. Each of them in their own way suffered from low self-esteem and poor self-image. This is a common theme found among women due to patriarchal cultural ideations, who suffer from depressive states for extended periods of time beyond the norm.

Three of the women had previously failed to get any help through allopathic antidepressant prescriptions. One of the major keys in their fast successful treatment was that through hypnosis and psychotherapy they were helped to mature their personalities and evolve a greater sense of self-efficacy. In this case the hypnotherapy was goal-focused, encouraged and fostered cognitive awareness and used both direct and indirect suggestion for behavioural change.

Recommendations

In order to help women in any kind of therapy it is necessary to afford them the time to deal with their concerns. GPs would be more effective if they referred patients complaining of depression to professionals specifically trained to deal with depression, exploring its emotional and biological causes rather than automatically administering unproven antidepressant pills. Hypnotherapy is the use of hypnosis with psychotherapy and the manipulation of the body's systems by suggestion for psychobiological change, particularly the endocrine system.

Hypnotherapy has proved itself time and time again to be one of the fastest and most cost-effective ways to address depression. In treating women who present with depression hypnotherapeutically, it is essential for the clinician to consider the women holistically to help change physical, psychological, spiritual, social, intellectual, sexual and economic concomitants of the whole woman.

Bibliography

Chang, J. *Wild Swans: Three Daughters of China.* London, England: Flamingo, 1993.

Beck, A. T. *The Diagnosis and Management of Depression.* Philadelphia, PA: University of Pennsylvania, 1973.

Breggin, P. *Toxic Psychiatry.* London: Harper Collins, 1993.

Crasilneck, H., and J. Hall. *Clinical Hypnosis: Principles and Applications.* Boston, MA: Allyn & Bacon, 1985.

Fuller Torrey, E. and M. B. Knable. *Surviving Manic Depression: A Manual on Bipolar Disorder for Patients, Families and Providers.* New York, NY: Basic Books, 2002.

Gauld, A. *A History of Hypnotism.* Cambridge, England: Cambridge University Press, 1992.

Greer, G. *The Female Eunuch.* London, England: Paladin Grafton Books, 1971.

Hodkinson, M. *As Tears Go By: Marianne Faithfull.* London, England:

Omnibus Press, 1991.

Holy Bible, The (King James Version). Peabody, MA: Hendrickson National Publishing Company, 2006.

Horlick, N. *Can You Have it All?* London, England: Macmillan, 1997.

Hornyak, L., and J. Green. *Healing from Within: The Use of Hypnosis in Women's Health Care.* Washington, D. C.: American Psychological Association, 2000.

Jensvold, M., U. Halbreich and J. Hamilton. *Psychopharmacology and Women: Sex, Gender & Hormones.* Arlington, VA: American Psychiatric Association Press, 1996.

Knight, S. *The Brotherhood: The Secret World of the Freemasons.* London, England: HarperCollins, 1994.

Laing, R. D. *Wisdom, Madness and Folly: The Making of a Psychiatrist.* London, England: Macmillan, 1985.

Metz, A. *Blondie: From Punk to the Present: A Pictorial History.* Springfield, MO: Musical Legacy Publications, 2002.

Moore, T. *Prescription for Disaster: The Hidden Dangers in Your Medicine Cabinet.* New York, NY: Simon & Schuster, 1998.

Miles, R. *The Women's History of the World.* London, England: Penguin, 1998.

Mitchell, S. *Kerryn & Jackie.* Sydney, Australia: Allen & Unwin, 2002.

Mosteshar, C. *Unveiled: Love & Death among the Ayatollahs.* London, UK: Hodder & Stoughton, 1995.

Paglia, C. *Vamps and Tramps.* London, England: Penguin, 1994.

Pope, A. *The Wild Genie: The Healing Power of Menstruation.* Bowral, Australia: Sally Milner Publishing, 2001.

Roddick, A. *Business as Usual.* London, England: Thorsons, 2002.

Rossi, E. *The Collected Papers of Milton H. Erickson on Hypnosis, vols. I–IV.* New York, NY: Irvington Publishers, 1989.

Sperry, L. *Diagnostic and Statistical Manual of Mental Disorders* Washington, D.C.: American Psychiatric Association. 1994.

Straffon, C. *The Earth Goddess: Celtic & Pagan Legacy of the Landscape.* London, England: Blandford, 1997.

Tuttle, L. *Encyclopaedia of Feminism.* Harlow, England: Longman Group, 1986.

Yapko, M. *Hypnosis and the Treatment of Depression: Strategies for Change.* Levittown, PA: Brunner/Mazel, 1992.

Internet References

Australian Bureau of Statistics. "Census of Population and Housing—The 2001 Census, Religion and the Jedi," Australian Bureau of Statistics. Retrieved March 2006 from http://www.abs.gov.au/websitedbs /D3110124.NSF/0/86429d11c45d4e73ca256a400006af80?OpenDocu ment

National Women's Justice Coalition. "Contribution on Articles 15 and 16 of CEDAW to the Australian Non-Government Organisations Report to the UN Commission on the Status of Women, Particularly in Response to the Australian Country Report," National Women's Justice Coalition. Retrieved March 2006 from http://www.nwjc.org. au/cedawrep.html

NSW Parliament. "Facts and Figures—Number of Women Members in the NSW Parliament, 1973 – 2003." NSW Parliament. Retrieved March 2006 from http://www.parliament.nsw.gov.au/prod/web/ common.nsf/key/ResourcesFactswomenmp3

"Aborigine Goddess Wuriupranili." Wikipedia: The Free Encyclopedia. Retrieved March 2006 from
http://en.wikipedia.org/wiki/Wuriupranili

DRU YOGA:
FROM DEPRESSION TO SELF-EMPOWERMENT

KIM DAVIS

Depression is one of the fastest-growing illnesses in the Western world and yoga one of the fastest growing self-help modalities, particularly among women. This essay discusses researched evidence supporting this correlation, explains the value of yoga for treating depression, and provides a focus on a particular form of yoga—Dru yoga, known for its gentle therapeutic movements and effectiveness in transforming negative emotional states (Barrington, Goswami & Jones, 2005).

Depression

Mental illness is one of the top ten leading causes of global disease (Murray & Lopez, 1996). In 1999 the Australian Institute of Health and Welfare listed Australia's top three health priority areas as cardiovascular health, cancer control and mental health, with a prediction that mental disorders will be the number one burden in Australia by 2020. There are many explanations for this serious increase in depression, including:

- **Social**—an increase in isolation and disconnection from family and community; abuse in many forms; terrorism and warfare. "Martin Luther King, Jr., observed that "our scientific power has out run our spiritual power. We have guided missiles and misguided men" (Sivaraksa, 2009: 20)
- **Psychological**—a sense of being unable to "keep up" with the constant technological changes in the world; "information overload" and a significant loss of traditional "values" and "meaning".
- **Spiritual**—Yogis have always believed that depression is caused by a sense of separation from our source—a disconnection from who we truly are and our life force.

- **Physical**—the body and brain need oxygen to function at optimal levels. Many of us are now sitting at desks or computers for many hours at a time with shoulders hunched forward, our breathing, chest and heart constricted. Less physical activity also means toxins and tensions usually flushed from the body with movement are left to stagnate, eventually resulting in illness.

- **Neurological**—National Institute of Health research indicates that anxiety and depression may be linked to lowered levels of neurochemicals in the brain, including dopamine, norepinephrine, serotonin and gamma-amniobutyric acid (GABA).

- **Emotional**—antidepressants are commonly prescribed to calm the stress response. In the UK alone, 97 percent of senior human resource professionals believe stress is the biggest threat to the future health of the workforce (Fuller, 2006) and yet perhaps stress and the emotions of depression are valid and appropriate in a world where millions of children die of poverty, the planet is in crisis, and imbalances and injustices prevail.

- **Global imbalance**—many are grieving global economic disparity, and the environmental degradation and devastating loss of fauna and flora species, habitats, indigenous cultures and balance with the ecosystems of planet earth: our home. Sulak Sivaraksa, a strong advocate for placing people ahead of profit, highlights that

20 percent of the world's population controls more than 80 percent of its wealth...one quarter of the world's population lives in the industrial North and consumes over 60 percent of the world's food, 85 percent of its wood and 70 percent of its energy. More than a billion people in the agricultural South live in absolute poverty, without access to the essentials needed for survival. (Sivaraksa, 2009: 82)

Of the 100 largest economies in the world, fifty-one are now global corporations; only forty-nine are countries (Anderson & Cavanagh, 2000). So corporations seeking profits are the driving force of global decisions today.

Sivaraksa argues that we try to overcome the emptiness of our lives by increased consumerism, brainwashed by advertising to believe "we need to become someone other than ourselves to have value" (Sivaraksa, 2009: 31). Yet yoga traditions teach the importance of reducing our desire for things. Mohandas Gandhi, a yogi, who rejected both the production and accumulation of material things, said "Mother Earth can well satisfy every living creature on it, but it can never satisfy even one person's greed" (Ibid.: viii). For many thousands of people, yoga is a form of spiritually based social activism, a means to re-value the interrelatedness of all; to address the deep grief of our planet and begin the healing.

Yoga has been shown to positively affect all these areas known to contribute to depression. Rather than turning the emotions of anger and despair inwards, yoga, and in my experience particularly Dru yoga, can assist in transforming depression to self-empowerment.

What is Yoga?

Yoga has been practiced on the Indian subcontinent for thousands of years as a systematic method for maintaining optimum physical, emotional, mental and spiritual health. Yoga involves three processes: movement, breathing exercises and relaxation (Gura, 2002) and is an ancient system for alleviating the human condition of suffering. The sacred text, *The Bhagavad-Gita*, believed to have been written 150 BCE, could be one of the earliest "medical journals" addressing depression. In the first chapter, the Lord Krishna explains to the depressed warrior Arjuna the "yoga" required to lift his spirit and fulfil his destiny.

Who's Doing Yoga?

Today, millions of people—particularly women—are finding yoga a safe, affordable and effective means of combating stress and depression. In late 1998 Stephen Penman published findings from the *Yoga in Australia Survey,* the largest survey of yoga in the world with 3836 respondents. Penman says:

> In the absence of any formal system of co-ordination or referral between the medical and yoga teaching professions, it seems that people are self-prescribing yoga for their health concerns. (Penman, 1998: 239)

Penman found more people used yoga to address mental health issues than physical problems (Ibid.). His research suggests people are increasingly looking outside the biomedical model for their healthcare because of a perceived lack of "wholism" in western medicine (Ibid.: 383) and the use of complementary therapies such as yoga is increasing. This trend is being "led by educated, professional women" (Ibid.: 382).

Recent studies reveal that 72.2 percent of women in the US practice yoga (*Yoga Journal*, 2008), while in Australia the percentage is even higher at 85.6 percent (Penman, 2009). The mean age of yoga practitioners in the US is 39.5 years old (Birdee, Legedza, Saper, Birtisch et al., 2008) and 41.4 years old in Australia (Penman, 2009).

Research from the US indicates that the number of people currently practicing yoga has more than doubled in the past ten years, from 7.4 to 15.8 million people, or from 3.8 percent to 6.9 percent of the population (Birdee et al., 2008; Saper, Eisenberg, Davis, Culpepper et al., 2008). In Australia, yoga participation has also grown rapidly in recent years. The Australian Bureau of Statistics has indicated that in 2003 over 300,000 people practised yoga over the preceding twelve-month period: this represented 2.5 percent of the population between the ages of twenty and seventy. In 2007, the Australian Sports Commission reported yoga use by 2.9 percent of the population, while other surveys indicate that yoga use could be as high as 7 to 12 percent of the Australian population (Penman, 2008).

Increase in Research

With the growing popularity of yoga, there has been an increase in medical and psychiatric research examining the effectiveness of yoga for relieving symptoms of depression. In his comprehensive *Survey of Yoga in Australia*, Penman provides a valuable table of forty-one significant research studies into the value of yoga and meditation in treating stress, anxiety, mood disorders and depression. In summarizing this research, he says:

> there is growing evidence in the literature supporting the use of yoga and meditation interventions for mental health issues such as stress, anxiety disorders and depression; primarily as adjunct therapies to conventional treatment or as part of a multidisciplinary approach, and occasionally as stand alone approaches. (Penman, 2008: 57)

Ned Hartfiel, a Dru yoga therapist, has concluded what is believed to be the first *Yoga in the Workplace* research study in the world and found that

> Dru yoga intervention resulted in significantly higher scores for the yoga group compared to the wait-list control group on seven of eight domains measured using the POMS-Bi and IPPA. (Hartfiel, 2008: 3)

In 2005 a study of a group of twenty-four emotionally distressed female participants who practiced yoga over twelve weeks were significantly less depressed/anxious and reported significantly more vigour than the control group who did not practice yoga (Michalsen, Grossman, Acil, Langhorst et al., 2005).

In 2004 yoga therapist Amy Weintraub published the best-selling *Yoga for Depression: A Compassionate Guide to Relieve Suffering through Yoga*, which became a valuable handbook for women everywhere. Weintraub is a Kripalu yoga teacher, and like teachers of Dru and other yoga styles, she offers clients suffering depression specific movements and breathing practices to: feel connected and grounded; balance the hemispheric function of the brain; energise the body and mind (when feeling sluggish and depressed); calm the body and mind (when feeling anxious and stressed); and develop a witness state or mindful awareness. Mindful awareness is the ability to observe and move through feelings and thoughts from a higher state without either becoming attached to or being defined by them.

Weintraub and her colleagues have completed a pilot study investigating the efficiency of the LifeFoce yoga program. Their results

> suggest participation in a comprehensive Yoga program, designed specifically to address mood, can lead to decreased symptoms of depression and associated physical or mood states. (Bennett, Weintraub & Khalsa, 2008: 49)

There is now rapidly growing researched evidence to support what yoga practitioners have known for centuries—that yoga can play an important role in improving and maintaining both mental and physical health:

> *Yoga* appears to be a promising intervention for *depression*; it is cost-effective and easy to implement. It produces many beneficial emotional, psychological and biological effects. [emphasis added] (Shapiro, 2006: 1)

Surveys of Yoga Practioners

In a study of yoga in the US, Birdee et al. found that 90 percent of their survey respondents who were currently practising yoga described the practice as "very helpful" or "somewhat helpful," especially for musculoskeletal conditions and mental health (Saper et al., 2004; Birdee et al., 2008). In Australia, 76 percent of yoga practitioners found it beneficial "to reduce stress and anxiety" (Penman et al., 2008).

In 2005 a survey of 440 Dru yoga practitioners (primarily in the UK and Australia) were asked thirty-four questions focusing on the perceived physical, mental and emotional benefits of Dru yoga practice. While many physical benefits were reported, those specific to mental health were:

- 89 percent found Dru Yoga helps them overcome stress;
- 93 percent were better able to handle negative thoughts;
- 83 percent had greater ability to handle their emotions;
- 84 percent experienced a positive shift in their mood;
- 73 percent gained a better ability to deal with conflict (Hartfeil 2008).

A number of yogic practices can not only help relieve depression but may put your students in touch with a deep source of joy and peace. (McCall, 2007)

How is Yoga Effective in Treating Depression?

The conventional wisdom holds depression to be a mood disorder.... It shows up in our self-defeating and addictive behaviours. It shows up in our thoughts as negative self-talk. It shows up in the way we perceive ourselves, others and the world. ...many of us live most of our lives mildly depressed. Separated—if you will—from our own (dare I say it) Life Force. (Cope, 2004: xi-xii)

Over sixty years ago the World Health Organisation (WHO) defined health as "a state of complete physical, mental and social wellbeing, and not merely the absence of disease or infirmity" (WHO, 1946: para. 1). Yoga encapsulates this definition. The word yoga is Sanskrit for yoke or join, and in yoga we assist people to reconnect or rejoin the "missing links" inside of themselves so they can reconnect with the world feeling integrated and whole.

Yoga also teaches the mind to yoke itself to the present moment (Forbes, Akturk, Cummer-Bnacco, Gaither et al., 2008). By learning to focus on the present, women with anxiety gain relief from concerns about future events and women with depression learn to disconnect from the past and recognize each new breath brings renewal and "life energy" (pranayama).

An ancient principle of yoga is that all aspects of the human being are inextricably linked. Yoga is designed to work with the physical, pranic/life-force, mental/emotional, intellectual and spiritual levels, recognizing all are interconnected, as part of the wholistic mind body spirit system. From a yoga perspective, an imbalance in any one of these layers or aspects will eventually manifest as illness in the physical body. We are also interconnected to all others on the planet and the global imbalances we are currently facing may well be a factor in the declining health of those sensitive to the disharmony.

Effective Forms of Yoga for Treating Depression

Since its introduction to the West, yoga has branched off into a variety of styles, each having a different "emphasis." As Hartfiel explains:

> the differences in yoga styles relate to how much focus there is on the alignment of the body, the coordination of breath and movement, the holding of postures, or the flow from one posture to another... All styles of yoga teach, to some degree, the three principle mechanisms of yoga: movement and postures, breathing techniques, and relaxation/meditation. (Hartfiel, 2008: 22)

The best type of yoga for depression depends partly on each individual's preference, personality and physical ability. However, recent research has examined Dru, Hatha, Iyengar, Kundalini, Kripalu, Lifeforce, Restorative and Viniyoga yoga styles, and all have shown to be beneficial in reducing stress and improving quality of life (Bennett, Weintraub & Khalsa, 2008).

More studies are needed to determine which styles and mechanisms are most effective in specific populations; however, researchers are finding that there are some common threads in the types of movements, breathing techniques and relaxations which provide the greatest benefit to those suffering depression.

Movements which invite the body to roll the shoulders back and open the chest and lungs are universally favoured, such as Bridge, Cobra, and Salute to the Sun. Movements which work directly with the lower three energy centres (chakras) are also proving to be beneficial (Sitting Forward Bend, Cat, Dog and Forward Bend) (Carter, 2002).

Breathing techniques which help breathing become deeper and slower, such as Diaphragmatic breath, or breathing which helps balance the mental and emotional systems, such as Alternate Nostril Breathing (*nadi shodhana*) or Right Nostril Breathing (*surya bhedanaare*) and practices that increase the length of inhalation relative to the exhalation are commonly taught across many yoga styles and other therapeutic modalities because changing our breathing pattern provides the most immediate change to how we feel.

Relaxation to activate the parasympathetic nervous system, allowing the body to achieve greater physical homeostasis and emotional balance is very helpful. Guided visualizations, mantras, chants and affirmations are also shown to be valuable.

Meditation may be beneficial for anxiety disorders in general, although people with a history of psychosis or personality disorder should seek the advice of a psychiatrist before commencing meditation (Bhargava,

2003). Meditation may also be contraindicated in depressive illnesses because of its introspective nature (Pittler & Wider, 2006).

Dru Yoga as Therapy

> By addressing clients' physical bodies along with thoughts and emotions, the practice of yoga can narrow the gap between insight and change. Yoga offers clients techniques that they can practice on their own and in relatively short time, outside of the context of therapeutic sessions. This gives clients a more active role in their healing process, reducing their dependency on the healthcare system and increasing their chances of remission.... Yoga therapeutics offers individuals with debilitating mental illness, who have long been dependent on the health care system, tools that can help awaken their own innate capacities for healing. (Forbes et al., 2008: 95)

I am a qualified Dru yoga therapist and have found Dru to be a safe and accessible form of yoga suitable for a wide range of ages and abilities. It is characterised by gentle flowing movements and therapeutic sequences, directed breathing, visualisation, and relaxation. Dru Yoga's energy block release sequences (EBRs) are shown to be effective for transforming negative emotional states (Barrington, Goswami & Jones, 2005). Dru yoga is recognised as a valuable form of yoga for healing trauma, and Dru yoga therapists have been offering workshops to health professionals and others working in war-torn countries around the world since 1995.

Dru yoga teachers undergo a two- to four-year training program and are certified by the International School of Dru Yoga. Professional competence is evaluated by written and teaching performance tests and assessed by senior teachers. The Dru yoga teacher training program is standardized throughout the world, which ensures best practice and reproducible results. Movements, breathing, relaxation and meditations are clearly outlined in student manuals and the therapeutic use for different conditions noted in theory and experiential training.

Dru Yoga is often called yoga of the heart because many of the postures and sequences are designed to work with the heart centre: this is a major factor in its therapeutic efficacy. In yoga, the heart chakra is known as the psychic centre of transformation. According to the Institute of HeartMath, California, the electrical field of the heart is sixty times greater than that of the brain (McCraty, Bradley &Tomasino, 2005). In Dru yoga, particular attention is directed to opening the heart centre before any attempt is made to release old emotions.

Eminent mind/body scientist Dr Dean Ornish's work shows that when we do not feel truly loved our immune system is compromised, increasing the rate of heart disease and cancer (Ornish, 1998). People with depression often describe feeling continually oppressed by the sensation of a "fist squeezing their heart" (Forbes et al., 2008: 88). In its position statement of 2003, the National Heart Foundation of Australia stated:

> There is strong and consistent evidence of an independent causal association between depression, social isolation and lack of quality social support and the causes and prognosis of coronary heart disease... furthermore the increased risk contributed by these psychosocial factors is deemed to be of similar order to the more conventional coronary heart disease risk factors such as smoking, dyslipidaemia and hypertension. (Bunker, Colquhourn, Esler, Hickie et al., 2003)

Clearly, women suffering depression may also be increasing their risk of developing other serious physical illness if untreated. Through the gentle work of Dru yoga, we Dru yoga teachers help people regain a sense of self-esteem and self-worth, and change these feelings of fear, loss and depression to creativity, compassion and self-empowerment.

Dru yoga teachers and therapists understand that sometimes when we experience long-term stress or emotionally traumatic incidents, particular systems or parts of the body become overloaded and a blockage occurs in the natural free flow of energy. The Chinese talk of chi and meridians of energy flowing throughout the body: in yoga these energy blocks are known in Sanskrit as *samskaras* and show up as strong sensation, numbness or a restriction in our emotional expression (Walters, 2002). These blocked emotions cause chemical changes in specific areas of our body and can eventually lead to both physical and mental illness.

Modern theorists such as Candace Pert, Professor of Physiology and Biophysics at Georgetown University Medical School, suggest that our physical body and our emotions are linked through neuro-peptides or "messenger molecules". We can become addicted to the state of emotion we are most used to, even if it's very painful and prolonged painful emotions prevent us from leading fulfilling lives (Pert, 1997).

A key feature of Dru yoga is the use of specially designed sequences which target the places in the body where emotions get trapped. These unique energy block release sequences and physical movements are enhanced by the use of breathing, hand gestures, affirmations, visualisation and relaxation techniques. After a short time of regular Dru yoga practice, people notice a marked improvement in how they think, feel and move.

An analogy often used in Dru yoga to describe depression is that of an oil lamp. Our base energy centre is like the reservoir of fuel. This fuel provides the energy required for the wick, or second energy centre, and when fuelled this wick produces the flame in the third energy centre. A depressed person may still have the fuel available to light the flame within, but the wick may be frayed or tangled, scattering or dissipating the energy. Simple Dru yoga movements and breathing patterns will help strengthen the second energy centre, allowing the flame of the solar plexus to be lit, and light to flow into the darkness of depression. "It is far better to light a candle than curse the darkness" (Chinese proverb).

Yoga philosophy describes five layers of our being. The most dense layer is the physical body, moving into the prana or energy layer which corresponds to our breathing. Next comes the emotional layer, and deeper still is the layer of intellectual thought. The fifth and deepest is the layer of soul-force or self-awareness.

This philosophy of the layering of being is not unique to Dru Yoga, and is described in many ancient yoga texts. However, in Dru Yoga, each layer is targeted directly and where possible simultaneously. This allows a healing transformation to take place more quickly (Walters, 2002).

When practicing Dru yoga, participants find that traumas, emotional distress and disempowering thoughts rise like bubbles through the layers of being, surfacing and being released very gently and slowly through the physical body (Ibid.). Yoga provides a valuable way for clients to access and release blocked emotional pain without the use of language.

> Most psychologists agree that the seeds for depression are sewn in infancy through patterns of relationships with significant others, prior to the acquisition of language. And research shows that when we suffer trauma it is mostly the lower, more primitive parts of the brain that are involved. According to Maryanna Eckberg, Ph.D., a psychologist who treats survivors of abuse, "A body-oriented treatment model speaks the language of these areas of the brain-sensation, perceptual experience, and somatic responses. Cognitive restructuring is, of course, important, but the healing process must also include bodily experience." (Weintraub, para. 12)

The ability to physically perfect a posture is also not all-important in Dru Yoga. Instead we focus on directing a client's awareness to their body/mind responses to the movements and reconnecting with self. All the sequences can be modified to suit any age or physical ability and this is particularly important when working with women suffering depression because body image and low self-esteem may be factors in whether they feel comfortable undertaking the movements at all.

In summary, Dru yoga is proving to be an effective tool for transforming depression because it:

- offers a self-help "tool-box" of techniques and skills to assist people manage and release the cause of the depression;
- is cost effective and easily accessible;
- offers a wholistic approach which integrates physical, mental, emotional and spiritual aspects of our being;
- is independent of culture, language or religion;
- is perfectly suited for any age, state of health or level of fitness;
- addresses the cause of depression rather than simply treating the symptoms with medication;
- complements counselling and other therapies;
- allows emotional hurts to be released without stirring up the past, or needing the use of language;
- encourages emotional intelligence, self-reliance and self-empowerment;
- helps glands and organs produce a healing chemical balance, improve circulation, and flush toxins from the body;
- reinforces positive beliefs and thinking patterns during relaxation, visualizations and meditation to invite the unconscious mind to relax and let go of any obstacles or blockages to health and happiness;
- balances the biochemistry of the brain;
- stimulates the endocrine system;
- reduces the activity of the sympathetic nervous system and to activate the relaxation response of the parasympathetic nervous system;
- dissolves negative or unsupportive thoughts and beliefs;
- brings the physical, mental and emotional body into balance, restoring a sense of well being and energy;
- recognises that the first thing a depressed person stops doing is moving, and Dru yoga therapists can tailor a specific program for each client—often starting with accomplishing just one or two easy movements regularly;
- requires only a floor, preferably a mat, sometimes a chair and cushion; and can be practised anywhere;
- encourages emotional clearing and physical cleansing of the lymphatic system;
- has many healing sequences available online, on DVD or CD so clients may work at home or one on one rather than attending a

class.

> I met Dru yoga at a time when I was worn out, burnt out and had finally reached the point when I knew I had to do something about the deep and re-occurring depressions that continually pulled me down. Meeting Dru yoga and the many inspired teachers gave me the tools to help myself and my whole life turned around. There is a deep healing wisdom in this approach to yoga and I can honestly say that I have not suffered depression or burn out since becoming involved. I now teach Dru yoga so that others can experience the same profound changes in their wellbeing and in their lives. ("S", Dru Yoga teacher, 2009)

How Can Health Professionals and Yoga Therapists Work Together in the Future?

Psychotherapy, medication and electroconvulsive therapy (ECT) are still the most common treatments for depression. The list of possible side effects from antidepressants is extensive (Forbes, 2008: 89) and many of those who are compliant with antidepressant regimens do not experience remission of symptoms (Nierenberg, Ostacher, Huffman, Ametrano, Fava & Perlis, 2008). When women with depression do not respond to medications or psychotherapy, ECT is used, which often results in cognitive impairment (Forbes 2008: 89). Fortunately, yoga is being more commonly prescribed to augment pharmacological treatments and as an effective complementary and alternative therapy. A national survey of Australian general practitioners (GPs) in 2007 found that 62 percent had referred or suggested patients use yoga and 65 percent had referred or suggested meditation to patients in the previous twelve months. The only therapies receiving a higher rate of referral or suggestion were massage (87 percent) and acupuncture (83 percent). About 10 percent of Australian GPs said they practiced yoga themselves (Penman, 2008: 32).

Janice Carter from Queensland University's Department of Psychiatry draws our attention to the fact that many of the tools used today in Cognitive Behaviour Therapy stem from yoga, such as: visualizations; breathing techniques; progressive muscular relaxation; mindfulness meditation and guided imagery. These practices have become well-established in mainstream clinical practice since the surge of interest in mind body therapies in the 1970s, and continue to prove effective in the treatment of depression (Carter, 2002).

A well-trained yoga teacher can provide clients with the full compliment of yoga movements, breathing and relaxation practices, a comprehensive and wholistic package, often at a lower cost to the client and the healthcare system. Indeed, in my experience, among yoga professionals and associations it is known that yoga teachers have already developed informal referral systems with healthcare professionals and are working in healthcare settings providing one-on-one consultancy services or specialized workshops as I have done.

As the burden on the healthcare system continues to rise and the evidence for the therapeutic benefits of yoga continues to increase, many more doctors, therapists and other healthcare workers around the world will choose yoga, and particularly Dru yoga, as the treatment of choice for most common mental health problems, says psychiatrist Dr. Helena Walters (2002). Dru yoga is a natural choice for:

- de-stress techniques for stress-related disorders, e.g. chronic fatigue, irritable bowel syndrome;
- de-traumatisation techniques for post-traumatic stress disorder;
- relaxation techniques for anxiety and phobic disorders;
- relaxation, breathing and specific posture sequences for depression;
- specific sequences and movements for emotional transformation e.g. fear, anger, guilt;
- programmes for managing addictive behaviour (Ibid.).

Dru yoga therapists are part of the international community of yoga professionals furthering research to develop the "best practice" models for treating depression. Future collaborative research may involve working with yoga practitioners and healthcare professionals with diverse styles and skill sets to bring together a range of movements and breathing patterns known to be effective.

> Ultimately, medicine has a single aim: to relieve human suffering. When measured against this benchmark, different therapies can be seen as effective or ineffective rather than "orthodox" or "unorthodox." No single professional group has ownership of health, and the best healthcare requires a multidisciplinary approach. Thus, there is an imperative for all healthcare professionals to work together for the benefit of their patients and the wider community. (Cohen, 2004: 645–6)

Yoga brings us home to the power and light within.
May we all shine brightly!

Resources

A range of Dru yoga CDs, DVDs and books providing instruction on Detraumatisation and Management of Emotional Pain are available from www.druyoga.com or http://www.druexperience.org. Author's website www.anahata-yoga.com.au/

Bibliography

Anderson, S., and J. Cavanagh. *Top 200: The Rise of Global Corporate Power*. Institute for Policy Studies. December 4th, 2000. http://www. corpwatch.org/article.php?id=377

Australian Institute of Health and Welfare. *Australian Burden of Disease and Injury Study*. 1999. http:/www.aihw.gov.au/publications/index. cfm/titile/5180

Barrington, C., A. Goswami and A. Jones. *Dru Yoga: Stillness in Motion*. Bangor, Wales: Dru Publications, 2005.

Bennett, S., A. Weintraub and S. Khalsa. "Initial Evaluation of the Lifeforce Yoga Program as a Therapeutic Intervention for Depression." *International Journal of Yoga Therapy*, 18 (2008): 49–57.

Bhargava, S. "Relationship of Meditation and Psychosis: Case Studies. *Australia and New Zealand Journal of Psychiatry* 37 (2003): 382.

Birdee, G., A. Legedza, R. Saper, S. Bertisch, D. Eisenberg and R. Phillips. "Characteristics of Yoga Users: Results of a National Survey." *Journal of General Internal Medicine* 23 no. 10 (2008): 1653–658.

Iyengar, B. K. S. *Yoga: The Path to Holistic Health*. London, England: Dorling Kindersley Limited, 2008.

Bunker, S. J., D. M. Colquhourn, M. D. Esler, I. B. Hickie, D. Hunt, V. M. Jelinek, B. F. Oldenburg, H. G. Peach, D. Ruth, C. C. Tennant and A. M. Tonkin. "'Stress' and Coronary Heart Disease: Psychosocial Risk Factors—National Heart Foundation of Australia Position Statement Update." *Medical Journal of Australia* 178 no. 6 (2003): 272–76.

Carter, J. *Yoga and Mental Health*. Presentation to the 37TH Annual Royal Australian College, Department of Psychiatry University of Queensland. 2002. http://www.therapywithyoga.com

Cope, S. "Foreword." In A. Weintraub, *Yoga for Depression*. xi–xiv New York, NY: Broadway Books, 2004.

Cohen, M. "Australasian Integrative Medicine Association." *Medical Journal Australia* 180 no. 12 (2004): 645–46.

Eckberg, M. *Victims of Cruelty: Somatic Psychotherapy in the Healing of Posttraumatic Stress Disorder.* Berkley, CA: North Atlantic Books, 2000.

Forbes, B., C. Akturk, C. Cummer-Bnacco, P. Gaither, J. Gotz, A. Harper and K. Hartsell. "Using Integrative Yoga Therapeutics in the Treatment of Comorbid Anxiety and Depression. *International Journal of Yoga Therapy*, no. 18 (2008): 87–95.

Fuller, G. "HR Fears for Employees' Health as Stress Grips Nation." *Personnel Today*, 12 September, 2006.

Gura, S. T. "Yoga for Stress Reduction and Injury Prevention at Work." *Work*, 19 no. 1 (2002): 3–7.

Hartfiel, E. "The Effectiveness of Dru Yoga for Reducing Stress and Enhancing Emotional Wellbeing in University Staff." Dissertation Bangor University, School of Healthcare Sciences. Bangor, 2008.

International Association of Yoga Therapists (IAYT). *Yoga for Depression.* 2008. http://www.iayt.org

Kraftsow, Gary. *Yoga for Wellness, Healing with the Timeless Teachings of Viniyoga.* New York, NY: Penguin/Arkana, 1999.

Khalsa, S. "Yoga as a Therapeutic Intervention." *Indian Journal of Physiology and Pharmacology*, 48 no. 3 (2004): 269–85.

McCall, T. *Yoga as Medicine: The Yogic Prescription for Health and Healing.* New York, NY: Bantam, 2007.

McCraty, R., R. T. Bradley and D. Tomasino. "The Resonant Heart." *Shift: At the Frontiers of Consciousness* 5 (2005): 15–19.

McDonald, A., E. Burjan and S. Martin. "Dru Yoga for Patients and Carers in a Palliative Day Care Setting." *International Journal of Palliative Nursing* 12 no. 11 (2006): 519–23.

Michalsen, A., P. Grossman, A. Acil, J. Langhorst, R. Ludtke, T. Esch, G. Stefano and G. Dobos. "Rapid Stress Reduction and Anxiolysis among Distressed Women as a Consequence of a Three-Month Intensive Yoga Programme." *Medical Science Monitor*, 11 no. 12 (2005): 555–61.

Murray, C. J., and A. D. Lopez. *The Global Burden of Disease: A Comprehensive Assessment of Mortality and Disability from Diseases, Injuries and Risk Factors in 1990 and Projected to 2020.* Global Burden of Disease and Injury Series, Vol. I. Cambridge, MA: Harvard School of Public Health, 1996.

National Institutes of Health (NIH). *Anxiety Webpage.* http://www.nih.gov

Nierenberg, A. A., M. J. Ostacher, J. C. Huffman, R. M. Ametrano, M. Fava and R. H. Perlis. "A Brief Review of Antidepressant Efficiency, Effectiveness, Indications and Usage for Major Depressive Disorder. *Journal of Occupational and Environmental Medicine*, 50 no. 4

(2008): 428–36.

Ornish, D. *Dr. Dean Ornish's Program for Reversing Heart Disease: The Only System Scientifically Proven to Reverse Heart Disease Without Drugs or Surgery*. New York, NY: Ballantine Books, 1990.

—. *Love and Survival*. New York, NY: Harper Collins 1998.

Pittler, E., and M. Wider. *The Desktop Guide to Complementary and Alternative Medicine*. St. Louis, MO: Mosby Elsevier Press, 2006.

Penman, S., M. Cohen, P. Stevens and S. Jackson. *Yoga in Australia: The Results of a National Survey*. Melbourne, Australia: RMIT University, 2008.

Pert, C. B. *Molecules of Emotion*. London, England: Simon and Schuster, 1997.

Pilkington, K., G. Kirkwood, H. Rampes and J. Richardson. "Yoga for Depression: The Research Evidence." *Journal of Affective Disorders* 89 (2005): 13–24.

Saper, R., D. Eisenberg, R. Davis, L. Culpepper and R. Phillips. "Prevalence and Patterns of Adult Yoga Use in the United States: Results of a National Survey." *Alternative Therapies in Health and Medicine*. 10 no. 2 (2004): 20–1.

Shapiro, D. *Yoga as a Complementary Treatment of Depression: Effects of Traits and Moods on Treatment Outcome*. Oxford, England: Oxford University Press. 2006. http://ecam.oxfordjournals.org/cgi/content/abstract/nel114v2

Sivaraksa, S. *The Wisdom of Sustainability—Buddhist Economics for the 21st Century*. Kihei, HI: Koa Books, 2009.

Smith, C., H. Hancock, J. Blake-Mortimer and K. Eckert. "A Randomized Comparative Trial of Yoga and Relaxation to Reduce Stress and Anxiety." *Complementary Therapies in Medicine*, 15 no. 2 (2007): 77–83.

Walters, H. *Dru Yoga for Transforming Emotional Pain*. Royal College of Psychiatrists, 2002. http://www.rcpsych.ac.uk/college/specialinterest groups/spirituality/publications.aspx

Weintraub, A. *Yoga for Depression: A Compassionate Guide to Relieve Suffering through Yoga*. Portland, OR: Broadway Books, 2004.

—. "Depression and our Forgotten Magnificence." Yoga.com website, 28 July 2004. http://www.yoga.com/ydc/enlighten/enlighten_document. asp?ID=325&section=9&cat=203

Woolery, A., H. Myers, B. Sternlieb and L. Zeltzer. "A Yoga Intervention for Young Adults with Elevated Symptoms of Depression." *Alternative Therapies in Health and Medicine*, 10 no. 2 (2004): 60–63.

Wolfson, N. "Incorporating Yoga." *Yoga Journal*, March/April (1999): 45–46.

World Health Organisation (WHO). *Constitution of First Principles.* New York, NY: WHO, 1946.

—. *WHO Definition of Health.* 1946. http://www.who.int/suggestions/faq/en/

—. *The Workplace: A Priority Setting for Health Promotion.* 2008. http://www.who.int/occupational_health

World Medical Organisation. "Declaration of Helsinki." *British Medical Journal*, 313 no. 7070 (1996): 1448–449.

Yoga Journal. "Yoga in America" Market Study. *Yoga Journal Releases 2008.* 26 February, 2008. http:// www.yogajournal.com

CHILDHOOD SEXUAL ABUSE AND DEPRESSION— CONNECTIONS, THEORIES AND PRACTICE IMPLICATIONS WITHIN THE PRIMARY CARE SETTING

SABIN FERNBACHER AND CHRISTINE HODGE

Introduction

Childhood sexual abuse is a significant issue for the Australian general population (as it is internationally), with one in three women and one in six men having such an experience (Mullen, Martin et al., 1996; O'Brien & Henderson, 2006). The most common reaction of victims/ survivors is depression and anxiety (Ferguson & Mullen, 1999). Primary care providers often work with people who suffer from depression, but are not always aware of the childhood sexual abuse history of their clients.

We want to take a look at these issues as well as some of the dilemmas concerning this area of work, such as "to ask or not to ask" at assessment. While one of the authors works in a specific team which resources and works in collaboration with primary care providers, we will attempt to provide a perspective on the issues that hopefully apply to a broader range of service providers within the primary care sector (and maybe beyond).

We will first provide some definitions of and data on childhood sexual abuse, and then provide an overview of the research on the impact of childhood sexual abuse on mental health (and more specifically the connection to depression). The next section will provide an overview and discussion of some of the practice issues as they relate to the primary care sector and provide some examples of discussion within the specific team that one of the authors manages. The final section of this article provides an overview of practice-related issues and some recommendations for good practice in this area of work.

While this article focuses on women, the authors wish to acknowledge that many men have also experienced childhood sexual abuse. While in the past males have mostly been excluded, in more recent years researchers have begun to include males and the impact of childhood sexual abuse to a greater degree. The area of providing sensitive services to males who experience depression and have a history of childhood abuse needs further exploration and a service system inclusive of their needs.

Childhood Sexual Abuse—Definition and Prevalence

A number of terms are used to talk about abuse of a sexual nature towards children: incest, rape, childhood sexual abuse, or assault. Some distinguish between non-contact sexual abuse, sexual abuse without penetration and sexual abuse involving penetration, while others do not clearly define the parameters of child sexual abuse (CSA). Another factor that influences the definition of what constitutes CSA relates to the age at which a person is considered to be a child. Some studies include children only up to twelve years old, while others include fifteen- or eighteen-year olds as children (the older age groups generally are related to the legal age for young people to engage in sexual activities); this inconsistency contributes to differences in prevalence rates. CSA is predominantly perpetrated by people known to the child rather than by strangers—and often occurs within a broader context of child abuse and/or family violence. The following are just two definitions of CSA:

> ...child sexual assault can include fondling genitals, masturbation, oral sex, vaginal or anal penetration by a penis, finger or any other object, fondling of breasts, voyeurism, exhibitionism and exposing or involving the child in pornography. (Australian Centre for the Study of Sexual Assault, 2005: 1)

> Child sexual assault occurs when someone uses a child or young person for their own sexual gratification....the abuse might include fondling, sexual exhibitionism, intercourse, oral or anal sex, masturbation in front of a child, photographing nude children, child prostitution. (Domestic Violence and Incest Resource Centre, 2001: para. 2)

The true extent of any type of interpersonal violence, such as family/domestic violence and sexual abuse, is difficult to determine. While national and international studies tend to rely on reported crimes, it has equally been established that reported crime data provide inadequate estimate of prevalence of such violence. Hence such data provide a conservative estimate of the true level of such abuse occurring in any society. CSA in particular remains underreported in comparison to other interpersonal violence (Fleming, 1997).

Notwithstanding these issues, available data are evidence of alarmingly high rates of CSA. The Australian part of the "International Violence Against Women Survey" established that 18 percent of women had experienced childhood sexual abuse (Mouzos & Makkai, 2004). Similar rates have been found by others: Fleming's study of a community sample of Australian women reports a 20 percent rate for CSA (1997) and a review of thirty studies found that between 15 to 30 percent of women had experienced CSA; this equates to one in three women having experienced such abuse (Ferguson & Mullen, 1999). Prevalence rates also vary depending on the setting or the sample population: for example, those accessing psychiatric inpatient units show higher rates (of all forms of interpersonal abuse) than community mental health samples, and these show higher rates than general population samples. Within the general population, incidence rates for girls vary between 6 to 62 percent, and a female-to-male ratio being that of twelve to one (Fleming, 1997; Weiss, Longhurst et al., 1998; Ferguson & Mullen, 1999).

Childhood Sexual Abuse—Impact

Child sexual abuse is thought to involve a disruption of the core person, often eventuating in affect tolerance difficulties, painful perceptions of self, problems in interpersonal relationships, and disrupted beliefs about oneself and the external world. (Neumann, 1994: 35)

A large body of research studies aim to examine the connection between CSA and the development of a mental illness in adult life. Similarly to Neumann, other researchers suggest that an experience of CSA constitutes a disruption of a child's sense of self, which can lead to difficulties in managing stressful situations and make the development of mental illness more likely (Herman, 1992; Molnar, Buka et al., 2001). The long-term sequelae of CSA includes a range of mental health/illness responses, including depression, anxiety, increased suicidality, as well as higher rates of mental illness in general—including Borderline Personality Disorder, Post Traumatic Stress Disorder, bi-polar and eating disorders, and alcohol/drug dependency (Muenzenmaier, Meyer et al., 1993; Briere & Elliott, 1994; Neumann, 1994; Neumann, Houskamp et al., 1996; Difede, Apfeldorf et al., 1997; Fleming, 1997; Gold, Lucenko et al., 1999; Dinwiddie, Heath et al., 2000; Paolucci, Genuis et al., 2001; Golding, 2002; Thompson, Crosby et al., 2003; Spataro, Mullen et al., 2004).

Depression is the display of a despondent mood or the loss of interest or pleasure in nearly all activities; irritability; sadness; changes in appetite or weight, sleep psychomotor activity; decreased energy; feelings of worthlessness or guilt; and difficulty thinking, concentrating, or making decisions. (Paolucci, Genuis et al., 2001: 22)

Depression and/or anxiety are the most commonly found (mental health) reactions to CSA by victims/survivors. A great number of studies have found this correlation between an experience of CSA and (adulthood) depression, anxiety, Post-Traumatic Stress Disorder and increased suicidality (Hall, Sachs et al., 1993; Muenzenmaier, Meyer et al., 1993; Briere & Elliott, 1994; Davidson, Hughes et al., 1996; Dinwiddie, Heath et al., 2000; Paolucci, Genuis et al., 2001; Read, Agar et al., 2001; Zlotnick, Mattia et al., 2001; Campbell, 2002; Ullman & Brecklin, 2002).

General population samples show higher rates of depression in those who have experienced CSA than those without such an experience (Weiss, Longhurst et al., 1998). Weiss and colleagues investigated twenty-one studies, including seven community studies, five non-clinical studies (college students) and nine clinical studies (psychiatric inpatients and outpatients), patients from general practice and patients waiting for a medical procedure. The general practice figures indicate that 83 percent of women with a history of CSA describe themselves as depressed, while only 32 percent of women who had no such experience describe themselves as depressed. Similarly, an Australian study undertaken within general practice settings show that almost 40 percent of women surveyed had experienced CSA before the age of sixteen (Mazza, Dennerstein et al., 1996). Weiss and colleagues (1998) also found that the length, severity and frequency of abuse are linked to the development of depression.

While not the focus of this article, it has also been established that an experience of CSA increases the likelihood of re-victimisation as adult (Mouzos & Makkai 2004; Australian Centre for the Study of Sexual Assault, 2005), with the risk for women doubling in adulthood if they have experienced CSA; this has been confirmed by other studies (Australian Bureau of Statistics, 1996).

Primary Care—The Context

The Primary Mental Health Teams (PMHTs) were initiated in the state of Victoria in 2001 and 2002 in response to the Victorian Government's priorities in Mental Health, which included:

supporting the Second National Mental Health Plan, improving access to mental health services, and developing a more inclusive and responsive mental health service system. The ultimate purpose of the intervention is to improve health for people with depression and anxiety through the enhancement of services delivered at a primary care level, particularly GPs and Community Health Counselors. (Day, Shrimpton & Hurworth, 2004: 3)

Prevalence in Primary Care Settings

The authors' involvement with a PMHT and awareness of the literature surrounding CSA and depression allowed for reflection on the anecdotal evidence that presented itself on the team in conjunction with the existing literature. The evidence seemed to suggest a high prevalence rate of CSA for women presenting with depression. This is not meant to suggest that CSA is a causal factor in depression; however, it does suggest that it may increase the risk of depression, just as it may increase the risk of anxiety, risk-taking behaviours, relationship difficulties, sexual fear, low self-esteem and PTSD (Fergusson & Mullen, 1999). Presentations discussed on the team seemed to be characterised by women who were making an initial disclosure of CSA and those who had disclosed on many occasions previously. Clinical discussions often reflected a large number of inconsistencies in relation to practise issues, which typically involved enquiry, privacy and confidentiality and intervention.

Given that the role of the PMHT is to enhance services delivered at a primary care level, the authors' reflection on these issues gave rise to examination of the prevalence rates of CSA and depression in non-clinical settings such as community and primary care settings, and more generally some of the practise issues that are associated with these settings.

As discussed above, the prevalence rates of CSA in clinical mental health settings is well documented and noted as consistently high, around 90 percent (Weiss, Longhurst & Mazure, 1999). The study by Weiss et al. (1999) in which they reviewed a number of studies indicated that the reported prevalence rate for CSA in women that were surveyed within community and college group settings ranged between 9 and 50 percent; this percentage increased to a range of 13 to 65 percent for depressed women with a history of CSA. The paper reported a much higher prevalence rate in the general practise setting; childhood sexual assault was reported at 57 percent and women with depression and a history of CSA at 83 percent.

As noted earlier there is extensive research that indicates a relationship between CSA and mental health problems, and Young, Read,

Barker-Collo and Harrison rightly stated that given the "diversity of psychiatric symptoms and diagnoses, routine enquiry by professionals seems critical to assessments and treatments" (2001: 408). This being said, both the literature and the experience on the PMHT indicate that there is a wide degree of variability among mental health professionals around enquiry. Studies consistently report under enquiry, with discrepancy rates ranging from 6 percent of spontaneously self-disclosure of sexual abuse where an enquiry is not specifically made, to 70 percent when specific enquiry about sexual abuse is made (Briere & Zaidi, 1989). Clearly, then, there is a disjuncture between what *should* be done and what *current practise is*. In order to clarify reasons for "not asking", we turned to the literature. Not surprisingly, there was a good deal of overlap between views held by clinicians on the PMHT and those expressed in the literature.

Barriers to Enquiry

The reasons for "non-enquiry" are typically referred to as "barriers to enquiry" by Read, Hammersley and Rudegeair (2007: 104), and "reasons for not enquiring" by Young et al. (2001). Listed below are a combined number of factors taken from both of these papers:

- other, more immediate concerns;
- concerns about offending or distressing clients;
- fear of vicarious traumatisation;
- fear of inducing "false memories";
- the client being male;
- client being more than sixty years old;
- client having a diagnosis indicative of psychosis;
- client is highly disturbed;
- strong biogenetic causal beliefs;
- clinician being male or opposite gender to client;
- insufficient time to respond to the enquiry;
- family members present;
- lack of training and confidence.

Reasons for Enquiry

The study by Young et al. (2001) suggests that most of these barriers are either unsubstantiated or a result of erroneous thinking. The main exception noted is where the client is highly disturbed or where there are other more immediate concerns, but even under these conditions it is not suggested that enquiry be abandoned; rather it suggested that it be delayed to a more appropriate time. Generally, there is overriding support throughout the literature for routine enquiry, with the main reasons underpinning this being:

- a demonstrated strong relationship between CSA and a range of mental health presentations (Briere & Elliott 1994; Cavanagh, Read et al., 2004);
- spontaneous disclosure of abuse being unlikely (Pruitt & Kappius, 1992);
- people being more likely to tell a mental health professional than anyone else (McCauley, E. Kern et al., 1997); and
- knowing a client has been abused enables accurate formulations, thorough suicide assessments and appropriate treatment plans (Young, Read et al., 2001).

In summary, the take-home message is that *non-enquiry* poses a risk of conveying a message that the abuse is unimportant (Bryer, 1922) and may represent collusion with society's denial of the prevalence and impact of CSA (Bryer, 1992; Doob, 1992). Consequently, for the reasons listed above and the summary statements, Agar and Read's (2002) argument that clinicians have an ethical responsibility to enquire about abuse seems particularly pertinent.

Mandatory Enquiry

When we accept that routine or mandatory enquiry should occur, a number of issues are raised and need to be addressed.

Screening. A commonly asked question in the literature is whether there should be "universal screening" or "case review screening" (Stevens, 2007)—that is, should all women be screened by their health professional, or should it be limited to those who are suspected to have experienced sexual violence? Stevens (2007) notes that case review tends to be a subjective method of screening that relies solely upon the judgement of the clinician, and as such can potentially overlook a number of survivors. Opinions in the literature are quite diverse on this matter; however, it does show that there is a high percentage of adult women who report that they would like health professionals to ask them about their present and past experiences of sexual violence (McAfee, 1995; Littleton, Berenson, & Breitkopf, 2007). It would seem, then, to be a logical conclusion that universal screening should take place, particularly in primary healthcare settings where it is known that women often present first (Holden, 2002) and on multiple occasions with sexual-violence-related health issues. Indeed, as Stevens (2007) suggests that routine inquiry about sexual abuse needs to become part of the way care is provided.

Everett and Gallop (2001) note that where mental health settings have moved to mandatory enquiry/screening, it has not always translated into the questions being asked, or information provided being used. Almost without exception this is due to mandated enquiry being introduced in the absence of staff training (Read & Fraser, 1998). There is a real danger that in uninformed or insensitive hands, enquiry may re-victimise survivors. We know that women who have experienced CSA may in late adolescence and adult hood experience:

- behavioural difficulties such as self-harm, suicide, dissociation and re-victimisation;
- physical difficulties where "their bodies have become their enemies" and the abuse is expressed through a multitude of somatic complaints;
- emotional difficulties in the form of affect dysregulation, fear, anger, despair and hopelessness; and
- relational difficulties particularly around abandonment and betrayal.

Therefore, knowledge, skill and sensitivity are required so that disclosure occurs in a supportive environment and is experienced as empowering for the client (Everett & Gallop, 2001). Screening then needs to be accompanied by workforce training: this is a necessary challenge where knowledge can be imparted, skills developed and sensitivity encouraged.

Privacy and confidentiality. In the course of discussion with PMHT, the issue of privacy and confidentiality was raised. The authors note that clinicians are often required to balance the need to record and incorporate women's experiences of CSA into diagnostic formulations with the development and maintenance of a safe and trusting environment. This is particularly so for women who experience relational difficulties. It would seem important that in order to avoid any re-traumatising in the form of violation of trust that a careful explanation is given regarding privacy and confidentiality. This explanation should include limits to confidentiality, particularly that records cannot always be protected and may be subject to court subpoenas. To the authors' knowledge there is little written in the literature that addresses this topic; however, Everett and Gallop do note that, "organisations should be clear on the legislation in their jurisdiction and have written policies on recording" (2001: 107). Having reflected on the literature, the authors suggest that this need not be an issue if, as Everett and Gallop suggest, clear information is provided to clinicians/healthcare workers in the course of their training and professional development, and this information is imparted to women in a trusting environment and in a clear and sensitive way.

Intervention. Finally we turned our attention to intervention. The issue regarding "use" of information provided through a disclosure was clear-cut on the PMHT. Consistent with the literature, it was viewed as essential for an understanding of the client's presentation, for the formulation and diagnosis, and to inform options for the most appropriate type of intervention. However, this response would seem to be at odds with the literature, where generally there would appear to be very low levels of response to disclosure (Read et al., 2007). Confidence in being able to provide an appropriate intervention may be one reason why response is so low. Confidence varied among clinicians on PMHT; some feel very confident in their ability to provide trauma therapy, while others do not have such skills.

The authors again drew on their knowledge of the literature and found that it makes a useful distinction between intervention at initial disclosure and ongoing intervention. Read, Hammersley and Rudegeair (2007) provide some useful guidance on how to respond at initial disclosure. They propose that the focus should be on the relationship with the client rather than on the abuse and that the clinician:

- affirm that it was a good thing to tell;
- do not try to gather all details;
- ask if the person has told anyone before (and how that went);
- offer support;
- ask whether the client relates the abuse to their current difficulties;
- check current safety (from ongoing abuse);
- check emotional state at end of session;
- offer follow up / check in (2007: 106).

This distinction is useful because clinicians do not need to be the experts (about sexual assault). They may provide the initial "safe environment" for disclosure to take place and then provide assistance and support for referral to a service or organization that can provide the ongoing intervention required to work through the issues associated with the CSA.

Development of Organisational Policy and Guidance

Organisational guidance, especially in the absence of a state-wide strategy or policy to direct mental health services in this area of work, can provide vital direction to become increasingly cognizant of the issue of sexual assault and the organisational responsibility to address these within clinical practice. The PMHT is part of an organisation, which has gone some way towards such development. One of the authors has been involved in the development and (local) implementation of a policy and associated guidelines called "For Abuse Inquiry and Response for Mental Health Workers"; both documents clearly state the organisational responsibility to provide enquiry and sensitive support to those clients who have experienced CSA. An associated training program provides the opportunity to enhance clinician's skills and confidence to work towards the implementation and follow-through of this policy to ultimately ask all clients of the mental health service about their sexual abuse history.

In summary, this paper is not intended as an exhaustive representation of the literature; rather, it seeks to deal with some of the practise issues encountered within primary care settings. In so doing it has identified that these issues are not limited to primary care settings, but are also experienced within specialist mental health settings. It highlights, however, that women will often present at primary health care settings in the first instance and may do so for sexual violence / health-related issues, and may do so on multiple occasions. This strengthens the argument that universal screening should occur and be repeated at regular intervals.

Acknowledgements

The authors wish to acknowledge and thank the members of the Primary Mental Health Team (Northern Area Mental Health Service), past and present, who have so generously shared their thoughts, knowledge and practice through discussions. The authors would especially like to thank Ms Robyn Humphries, manager of NAMHS, for her ongoing support, encouragement and her vision!

Bibliography

Australian Bureau of Statistics. "Women's Safety Australia." Canberra, Australia: Commonwealth of Australia, 1996.
Australian Centre for the Study of Sexual Assault. "Adult Victims/Survivors of Childhood Sexual Assault." ACSSA Wrap. 2005.

Retrieved 22 March 2006 from http://www.aifs.gov.au/acssa/pubs/wrap/w1.hmtl

Briere, J., and D. Elliott. "Immediate and Long-Term Impacts of Child Sexual Abuse." *The Future of Children* Vol. 4 no. 2 (1994): 54–69.

Campbell, J. C. "Health Consequences of Intimate Partner Violence." *The Lancet* Vol. 359 no. 9314 (2002): 1331.

Cavanagh, M.-R., J. Read, et al. "Sexual Abuse Inquiry and Response: A New Zealand Training Programme." *New Zealand Journal of Psychology*, Vol. 33 no. 3 (2004): 137–44.

Davidson, J. R., D. C. Hughes, et al. "The Association of Sexual Assault and Attempted Suicide within the Community." *Archives of General Psychiatry* Vol. 53 no. 6 (1996): 550–55.

Day, N., B. Shrimpton and R. Hurworth. *Evaluation of the Primary Mental Health and Early Intervention Initiative.* Baseline Report for the Department of Human Services, Victoria, Australia, 2004.

Difede, J., W. Apfeldorf, et al. "Physical and Sexual Abuse During Childhood and Development of Psychiatric Illnesses during Adulthood." *Journal of Nervous & Mental Disease* Vol. 185 no.8 (1997): 522–24.

Dinwiddie, S., A. Heath, M. Dunne, K. Bucholz et al. "Early Sexual Abuse and Lifetime Psychopathology: A Co-Twin-Control Study." *Psychological Medicine*, Vol. 30 no. 1 (2000): 41–52.

Domestic Violence and Incest Resource Centre. "Childhood Sexual Abuse: Information for Adults Who Have Experienced Abuse as a Child." 2001. Retrieved 31 August 2005 from http://www.dvirc.org.au/publications/Incest.htm

Ferguson, D. M., and P. E. Mullen. *Childhood Sexual Abuse: An Evidence-Based Perspective.* London, England: Sage, 1999.

Fleming, J. M. "Prevalence of Childhood Sexual Abuse in a Community Sample of Australian Women." *Medical Journal of Australia*, 166 (1997): 65–8.

Gold, S. N., B. A. Lucenko, et al. "A Comparison of Psychological/Psychiatric Symptomatology of Women and Men Sexually Abused as Children." *Child Abuse & Neglect* 23 no. 7 (1999): 683–92.

Golding, J. "Inscribed Bodies: Health Impacts of Childhood Sexual Assault." *Medscape General Medicine* 4 no. 4 (2002):

Hall, L. A., B. Sachs, et al. "Childhood Physical and Sexual Abuse: Their Relationship with Depressive Symptoms in Adulthood." Image: Journal of Nursing Scholarship 25 no. 4 (1993): 317–23.

Herman, J. "Trauma and Recovery." New York, NY: Basic Books, 1992.

Mazza, D., L. Dennerstein, et al. "Physical, Sexual and Emotional Violence against Women: General Practice-Based Prevalence Study." *Medical Journal of Australia*, 164 (January, 1996): 14–7.

McCauley, J., D. E. E. Kern, et al. "Clinical Characteristics of Women with a History of Childhood Abuse: Unhealed Wounds." *The Journal of the American Medical Association*, 277 no. 17 (1997).

Molnar, B., S. Buka, et al. "Child Sexual Abuse and Subsequent Psychopathology: Results from the National Comorbidity Survey." *American Journal of Public Health* 91 no. 5 (2001): 753.

Mouzos, J., and T. Makkai. "Women's Experience of Male Violence: Findings from the Australian Component of the International Violence against Women Survey." Canberra, Australia: Australian Institute of Criminology, 2004.

Muenzenmaier, K., I. Meyer, et al. "Childhood Abuse and Neglect among Women Outpatients with Chronic Mental Illness. [see comment]." *Hospital and Community Psychiatry* 44 no. 7 (1993): 666–70.

Mullen, P. E., J. L. Martin, et al. "The Long-Term Impact of the Physical, Emotional and Sexual Abuse of Children: A Community Study." *Child Abuse & Neglect* 20 (1996): 7–21.

Neumann, D. A. "Long-Term Correlates of Childhood Sexual Abuse in Adult Survivors." *New Directions in Mental Health Services* 64 (Winter 1994): 29–38.

Neumann, D. A., B. M. Houskamp, et al. "The Long-Term Sequelae of Childhood Sexual Abuse in Women: A Meta-Analytic Review." *Child Maltreatment* 1 no. 1 (1996): 6–16.

O'Brien, B., and K. Henderson. "Reframing Responses: Improving Service Provision to Women Survivors of Child Sexual Abuse who Experience Mental Health Problems—Report and Recommendations." Sydney, Australia: University of Sydney & Mental Health Coordinating Council, 2006.

Paolucci, E. O., M. L. Genuis, et al. "A Meta-Analysis of the Published Research on the Effects of Child Sexual Abuse." *Journal of Psychology* 135 no. 1 (2001): 17–36.

Pruitt, J. A., and R. E. Kappius. "Routine Inquiry into Sexual Victimization: A Survey of Therapists' Practices." *Professional Psychology, Research and Practice* 23 no. 6 (1992): 474–79.

Read, J., K. Agar, et al. "Assessing Suicidality in Adults: Integrating Childhood Trauma as a Major Risk Factor." *Professional Psychology: Research and Practice*, 32 no. 4 (2001): 367–72.

Spataro, J., P. E. Mullen, et al. "Impact of Child Sexual Abuse on Mental Health: Prospective Study in Males and Females." *British Journal of Psychiatry* 184 no. 5 (2004): 416–21.

Thompson, K., R. Crosby, et al. "Psychopathology and Sexual Trauma in Childhood and Adulthood." *Journal of Traumatic Stress* 16 no. 1 (2003): 35–8.

Ullman, S. E., and L. R. Brecklin. "Sexual Assault History and Suicidal Behaviour in a National Sample of Women." *Suicide & Life Threatening Behaviour* 32 no. 2 (2002): 117–30.

Weiss, E. L., J. G. Longhurst, et al. "Childhood Sexual Abuse as a Risk Factor for Depression in Women: Psychosocial and Neurobiological Correlates." *American Journal of Psychiatry* 156 no. 6 (1998): 816–28.

Young, M., J. Read, et al. "Evaluating and Overcoming Barriers to Taking Abuse Histories." *Professional Psychology: Research and Practice*, 32 no. 4 (2001): 407–14.

Zlotnick, C., J. Mattia, et al. "Clinical Features of Survivors of Sexual Abuse with Major Depression." *Child Abuse & Neglect* 25 no. 3 (2001): 357–67.

DEPRESSION IN AFRICAN WOMEN

MAGNOLIA BAHLE NGCOBO
AND BASIL J. PILLAY

Abstract

The prevalence of depression among African women in South Africa is considered to be high. The lack of and grossly inadequate psychological services resulting from past racial discriminatory laws of apartheid and a plethora of present day factors associated with a society in transition contributes to the continued under-reporting or misdiagnosing of the disorder in this group. In addition, the distinctive cultural factors and worldview of African woman also affect how depression is presented and/ or understood. The objective of the study was to understand depression in African women attending a health service.

Clinical records of female patients presenting with depression at a general hospital in a densely populated African township were examined over a two-year period. A review of the biographical and epidemiological data of these patients is presented. Depression in these women was related to socioeconomic factors, such as poverty, overcrowding, unemployment, high levels of crime, lack of services and abuse—to a considerable degree a relic of the past discriminatory apartheid system.

The conclusions that follow emphasize that these women return to a social context within which depression is increasingly prevalent. Recommendations are made for establishing psychological services relevant to their needs as well as means of ensuring that therapeutic gains extend to their social context.

Introduction

It is generally understood that twice as many women suffer from depression than men (Rapmud & Moore, 2000) and it is considered to affect one in five women (South African Depression and Anxiety Group,

2006). Little is understood about the significant gender deference in depression.

It is also important to distinguish between depressive symptoms and a depressive disorder. Depressive symptoms can be detected by many useful scales such as the Beck Depression Scale (Beck, Steer, & Brown, 1996), Hamilton's Depression Scale (Hamilton M, 1967) or the Zung Self-Rating Depression Scale (Zung, 1965). A depression disorder implies a formal psychiatric diagnosis based on a systematic comparison of the individual's mental health history and his or her signs and symptoms with predetermined criteria, such as the Diagnostic and Statistical Manual, fourth edition, text revised—DSM-IV-TR (APA, 2005).

In South Africa, diagnosing and treating clinical depression and recognising depressive symptoms, particularly among African people, plagues all mental-healthcare providers. Although there are a few studies which have shown that black South African women experience higher rates of clinical depression (Mkhize & Mayekiso, 1993; Robertson, Allwood & Gigiano, 2003), very little is understood about depression in African women.

One of the reasons for the poor understanding of depression in African women may be because we think and speak about depression in African women in the same way that we do among other race and gender groups, assuming that it follows the same pattern in all cultural groups. Another issue is that prevalent data regarding depression in black South African women are either non-existent or tentative, because past published clinical research on depression in black South African women has been scarce (Kane & Lowis, 1999; Jones-Webb & Snowden, 1993; Mkhize & Mayekiso, 1993). While there was no value seen under apartheid to study depression and or condition in black women, this scarcity is in part also due to the fact that black South African women may not seek treatment for their depression and may be misdiagnosed, or may withdraw from treatment because their ethnic, cultural, and/or gender needs have not been met (Swartz, 1998; Lund & Swartz, 1998).

A diagnosis of clinical depression in black women may also be missed due to the use of a different discourse related to its causes, symptom presentation and management. Formal scholarly discourse which informs theory and practice in South Africa excludes certain African concepts and world views. Two key factors contribute to the misdiagnosing and mismanaging of depression in black South African women. The firstly has to do with language. Translation from English to an African language is not easy. A specific term in isiZulu may refer to different states or condition in English, or may not have an equivalent. For example, the word *oluhlaza* can mean both green and blue. Terms have to be elaborated and described. In many cases, English terms referring to different symptoms and emotional states have no equivalents in African languages. For example, "feeling blue" in the English language is associated with certain emotional states; this is not the case in isiZulu, and such an item is meaningless if literally translated. On the other hand, *kubuhlungu inhliziyo* is a popular Zulu idiom referring to emotional pain or being disappointed. When literally translated, it means that "I have pain in my heart". Thus depressive symptoms in black African patients are not easily or accurately detected on depression inventories or measures.

Secondly, possible differences in symptom presentation may affect the way depression is recognized and diagnosed among black South African women. For example, most black women are more likely to report somatic symptoms, such as appetite change and body aches and pains, rather than report how they feel. In addition, there are few available culturally competent researchers who are knowledgeable about the phenomenon of depression in black South Africans, let alone African women. Furthermore, black South African women may not be willing to participate in research. This paper is intended to highlight some of the issues of depression in so far as they pertain to African women.

Method

The study was conducted at a general hospital situated in one of the densely populated black townships in KwaZulu-Natal, South Africa. The township and the hospital are surrounded by informal settlements (squatter camps) and small government-provided starter houses. The majority of the population seen at the hospital is Zulu-speaking. The principal investigator was a qualified clinical psychologist providing psychological services at the hospital. The study was purely exploratory and descriptive, involving a retrospective survey of clinical records of all patients who presented to the psychology clinic from the beginning 2004 to the end of 2005. All patients were first medically screened by a medical practitioner, psychiatry registrar or psychiatrist before being referred to the clinical psychologist because of symptoms of depression.

In total, eighty-eight patients' clinical files referred for depression were identified. Thirty-four were excluded because of missing data. Of the fifty-four clinical files that remained, a further twelve were excluded (one Indian, one white and ten male patients), so as to focus exclusively on black African women. The final sample was N = 42. In addition to data in the files, traditional African perceptions and attitudes about depression and mental illness were also gathered.

Results

The country's previous practice of racial segregation of the health services significantly contributed to the high African attendance at the hospital. Hence, before exclusively selecting the African women for the study, of those seen for depression over the two year period, fifty-two were black (96.30 percent), one Indian (1.85 percent) and one white (1.85 percent); among the black population (96.30 percent), only ten were males (19.23 percent)—forty-two were female (80.77 percent). The ratio of African female to male patients was four to one.

The ages of the African women in the sample ranged from seventeen to sixty-nine years, with a mean of 34.40 (SD 11.72). Their mean level of education was Grade 9.09 (SD 3.56), with the median being Grade 10 and mode Grade 12. Most were unemployed (thirty-two—76.19 percent). Thirty (71.43 percent) had no further education or training. With regards to marital status, twenty-nine were single (69.05 percent), eight married (19.05 percent), three widowed (7.14 percent) and two divorced (4.76 percent). See Table 1 above.

While the majority of the patients cited stress as the cause of the depression (thirty-five, 83.34 percent), those with no formal education or only primary schooling were more likely to cite bewitchment and failure to perform some traditional ritual. Based on Diagnostic and Statistical Manual of Mental Disorders (DSM-IV) criteria, the highest number of patients were diagnosed with a depressive disorder (thirty-eight, 90.47 percent). The majority of the patients lacked actual and perceived support (thirty-eight, 90.37 percent) with immediate family being a support for fifteen patients (35.71 percent) and the church for one (2.38 percent).

Psychosocial factors, such as unemployment, lack of finances and relational problems, predominated. However, there were other specifically identified stressors. These include experiences of losing someone through death (26.19 percent), domestic violence and abuse, and HIV-related factors. The average number of sessions attended was 1.83 (SD1.92) with a median of 1.

Table 6.1. Factors Associated with African Women Seen for Depression

	n (percentage)
Employment Status: Unemployed	32 (76.20)
Education	
No education	3 (7.14)
Primary education	8 (19.05)
High school	31 (73.80)
Marital Status	
Unmarried (single)	29 (69.05)
Married	8 (19.05)
Divorce	2 (4.76)
Widowed	3 (7.14)
Aetiology	
Stress	35 (83.34)
No reason	1 (2.38)
Traditional (bewitchment, role of the ancestors, calling to be a sangoma)	4 (9.52)
DSM IV-TR Diagnosis	
Mood Disorder (MDD / Dysthmia)	38 (90.47)
Acute Stress Disorder	1 (2.38)
Schizoaffective Disorder	1 (2.38)
Somatoform Disorder	2 (4.76)
Stressors	
Death in family	11 (26.19)
HIV-related	9 (21.43)
Sexual abuse	6 (14.28)
Domestic violence/ abuse	6 (14.28)
Unfaithfulness	5 (11.90)
Support structures	
None	38 (90.37)
Immediate family	15 (35.71)
Church	1 (2.38)

Table 6.2. Common Presenting Symptoms

Symptom	n (%)
Pain (including headaches)	35 (83.33)
Headache	20 (47.62)
Insomnia	27 (64.28)
Tearfulness	19 (45.24)
Suicidal behaviour	18 (42.86)
Loss of appetite	12 (28.57)
Depressed mood	13 (30.95)
Low energy	11 (26.19)
Poor memory	8 (19.05)
Unhappy	7 (16.67)
Poor concentration	7 (16.67)
Poor performance	6 (14.28)
Isolates self	5 (11.90)
Auditory hallucinations	5 (11.90)
Weakness / Fainting spells	5 (11.90)

Pain ranging from generalised pain to specific pain was the most common symptom reported (83.33 percent) of which headache was the most frequent (47.62 percent). The next most common symptoms were insomnia (64.28 percent), tearfulness (45.24 percent) and suicidal thoughts (42.86 percent). Table 2 lists other common symptoms.

Older patients were more likely to report their depression as a form communication with the ancestors. They usually consulted a traditional healer to help them "treat" their illness and to perform the necessary rituals. More than 40 percent of the patients had consulted a traditional healer prior to the primary health care practitioners and continued to use both traditional and western forms of treatment.

Those that provided traditional explanations unanimously agreed that depression "as diagnosed by western doctors" is foreign to the African world view. Like other mental illnesses, the African view of a person with depression is considered: bewitched (*uthakathiwe*); possessed by the spirits (*uyathwasa*); neglected to perform certain rituals resulting in his ancestors' discontent (*idlozi lidiniwe*), or laziness (*uyavilapha*).

It was also reported that depression in the African community is often not a primary concern and is therefore ignored. The reason for this is that the majority of patients live in poverty and struggle with complex socioeconomic issues: most of their time and energy is directed towards attending to basic needs such as food, housing, and employment, for themselves and their families, which take "priority" over depression.

Participants also felt that most African families believed that depression would be resolved in time on its own, and that the support and the sense of closeness of the extended family and neighbours often showed towards the depressed person were important. In addition, they believed that once a ritual was performed the depressed person would resume normal functioning.

Discussion

This study lends support the view that depression in black South African women is high (83.34 percent), that there is a gender difference (four to one), and is associated with low socioeconomic factors, loss through death and abuse. There is a high somatic presentation associated with the disorder.

It is unfortunate that although the women in this study had achieved a reasonable level of education, the socioeconomic factors and culturally expected responsibilities appear to restrict and prevent them from breaking out of this oppressed context. Being single and lacking both social support and financial independence may account for the high levels of domestic violence and abuse that these women experience and the high HIV-related problems. Lack of resources leaves these women with no alternative but to remain in abusive relationships and at risk for HIV and AIDS.

Another finding in this study which is in keeping with other studies on depression in African women nationally and internationally is that a high number of patients reported physiological pains to the health practitioners, more so or over and above mood symptoms. This is an important issue which often leads to poor detection of depression, particularly at the primary care level. Even in developed countries, research has shown that only a minority of primary care patients with depression received specific mental health treatment. In South Africa it has been found that thousands of patients with mental health problems are not diagnosed at the primary health care level (Pillay, Naidoo & Lockhart, 1999) or at visits to their general practitioners (Pillay & Cassimjee, 2000).

The patients in this study lacked social support. Support is an important factor in black women's responses to stress. The importance of a supportive environment in healing has been long recognized in black communities (Swartz, 1998). This lack of support leaves the women vulnerable to a wide range of stressful events such as violence, abuse, etc.

An alarming finding is that on average the patient attended one session. Given the evidence-based intervention practices in the treatment of depression, such as cognitive behavioural therapy and antidepressants, several sessions are required in order to successfully treat these patients. The inability to attend more than a single session is a direct consequence of other important factors competing for their time and meagre resources. This was expressed by a participant who stated that depression was not considered a "serious condition given all the other more serious problems they have to deal with" and the perception that it will resolve on its own accord.

Even though a high number of patients (83.34 percent) indicated stress as an aetiology for their depression, traditional beliefs and cultural understanding of the disorder contributes to the way help-seeking takes place and adherence. As many as 40 percent indicated that they had consulted a traditional healer.

Traditional treatment, according to Ngubane (1977), is provided by the *inyanga* (a traditional doctor) and *isangoma* (diviner). The *inyanga*, usually a man, must first serve an apprenticeship for a period not less than a year. Sometimes the skill is passed from a father to a son who shows an interest in traditional medicine. The *isangoma*, usually a woman, is required to have a comprehensive knowledge of traditional medicine. A person is "called" or chosen to be an *isangoma* by the ancestors who bestow special powers on the individual. In addition to the *inyanga* and the *isangoma*, there are those who prepare medicines for a particular type of illness or possess knowledge on how to deal with particular health related situations—they are known as the *inyanga* of a particular disease or condition, for example, *inyanga yomhlabelo*—the doctor who handles fractured bones. These are the equivalents of specialist healers. Traditional healers play a central role in African rural communities and their influence is fairly extensive among both industrialised and urban communities as well. It generally accepted that these traditional healers are usually consulted first.

With the rise and development of the indigenous churches, a new type of healer has emerged—the "prophets" or "faith healers" (*umthandazi*). They use both traditional methods as well as "Christian approaches" in their treatments. The main differences between "faith healers" and "traditional healers" are that these prophets are Christians who are church leaders: they pray and use holy water, and the sacraments of baptism, the Eucharist and unction, whereas diviners use traditional herbs, bones and medicines (Wessels, 1987b, 1989). The prophets maybe less knowledgeable about the "sickness" that is specific to the African culture compared to the traditional healers. In addition to healing those who have suffered misfortune, faith healers minister to those who suffer from schizophrenia, epilepsy, mental retardation, and inherited disorders.

According to Wessels (1987b), faith healers play a very useful role in the African community in handling day-to-day problems of living. The fact that the African Independent Churches are the fastest growing religious movement in Africa indicates the extent of their success in African societies (Oosthuizen, 1986).

In addition to rituals such as dancing, calling up the spirits of the ancestors and bone throwing (Ngubane, 1977; Wessels, 1985c), medicines are also administered. These are usually made from leaves, bark, roots stems, bulbs, fruit and/or seeds that are either fresh or dried and sometimes powdered. These medicines are often boiled and taken orally. The herbal medicines are divided into those that have healing properties and those that are used in rituals and have symbolic meaning. This latter group is usually used as prophylactics or to remove the cause of illness rather than to cure organic symptoms. Faith healers use prayer and holy water (*iziwasho*) for this purpose.

Sometimes these medicines are used as purgatives, usually to reduce excess gall which is believed to be the cause of stomach disorders. Purgatives are also taken in the form of an enema. It is believed that the purgatives clean out the cause of the illness. This practice, however, has often contributed to irreparable physical damage, and even death. In the hospitals it is a very common experience to find children and adult seriously ill as a result of the use of purgatives. Various lethal substances are used as enemas: the most common are Jeyes Fluid (a disinfectant), detergents, battery acid and potassium permanganate, which are believed to have cleaning properties. Sometimes the herbs that are used are extremely poisonous. Another common treatment method is the steaming method (*ukugquma*). It is also believed to have a cleansing effect and is often prescribed together with the enema and emetic.

Black patients regularly seek both traditional and western treatments concurrently without informing either practitioner—and the simultaneous use of both prescribed treatments may at times be contraindicated.

The results in this study mirror the experiences of African-Americans (Das et al., 2006). These authors found that African-Americans face a number of barriers in the recognition and treatment of major depression including clinical presentation with somatisation, stigma about diagnosis, competing clinical demands of co-morbid general medical problems, problems with the physician-patient relationship, and lack of comprehensive primary care services. They conclude that African Americans who have depression may be frequently under-diagnosed and inadequately managed in primary care as a result of patient, physician, and treatment-setting factors.

Conclusion

South Africa has a population of 48.7 million, of which 52 percent (approximately 25.2 million) of the population is female (Statistics South Africa, 2008). The black African population in the country is 38,565,100, of which 20,037,100 are female. Given that this group is more represented in the nation's lower socioeconomic strata than any other population group, has chronic medical problems and limited access to health services, black South African women are prominent targets for clinical depression. Depression is debilitating because it interferes with the essential functional abilities of an individual, thwarts productivity, and can increase the risk for other severe health problems (Robertson et al., 2003).

These results also have serious ramifications for health service planning and effective intervention strategies. Addressing this situation even conservatively will require serious inter-sectorial restructuring at several levels. The social and economic status of black women has to be critically addressed. Poor or minimal treatment and returning these individuals to similar socioeconomic contexts will not have any impact on the treatment of their illness.

There has to be inter-sectorial collaboration. Health has to also be radically revised and transformed to cope with the barriers patients face in seeking help. In order to improve access, treatment has to be free, flexible to accommodate the consumer, and employers and other stakeholders should participate in improving adherence and removing help-seeking barriers. A revision of the nomenclature of disorders is necessary and the training of health workers must ensure that they are equipped to attend to individuals and groups in diverse cultural contexts. There is a need to rigorously challenge a psychological practice based almost exclusively on dominant Western conceptualizations of mental health. In addition, the health services need to focus on preventive strategies as well as curative care. The pervasive situation requires training of all healthcare practitioners from the primary level care to identify and provide culturally appropriate intervention.

Given that most African women are single parents, heads of households with young dependent children, and have poor social support, involving community and faith-based organisations are essential. Prevention strategies must begin at school level so as to provide children and adolescents with appropriate skills and knowledge in areas such as improving self-confidence and enhancing self-esteem at an early age in order to break this ubiquitous cycle. Education and skill-building in stress reduction, problem-solving techniques, and psycho-education should be emphasised.

Note

The terms Black, African, White, Indian and Coloured refer to the previously used classifications of apartheid groupings and are not used in this paper to support racist discourse; rather, they are used to highlight the gaps that exist in the research in psychology.

Bibliography

American Psychiatric Association. *Diagnostic and Statistical Manual of Mental Disorders-IV-TR*. Arlington, VA: APA, 2005.

Berglund, A. I. *Zulu Thought Patterns and Symbolism*. Cape Town, South Africa: David Phillips, 1976.

Beck, A., R. Steer and M. Garbin. "Psychometric Properties of the Beck Depression Inventory: Twenty-five Years of Evaluation." *Clinical Psychology Review,* 8 (1988): 77–100.

Bhatia, S. C., and S. K. Bhatia. Depression in Women: Diagnostic and Treatment Considerations. *American Family Physician* (1999): 166–178.

Breznitz, Z. "Verbal Indicators of Depression." *The Journal of General Psychology* (2001): 351–363.

Das, A. K., M. Olfson, H. L. McCurtis and M. M. Weissman. "Depression in African-Americans: Breaking Barriers to Detection and Treatment. *Journal of Family Practice,* 55 no. 1 (2006): 30–39.

Edwards, D., and E. Besseling. "Relationship between Depression, Anxiety, Sense of Coherence, Social Support, and Religious Involvement in a Small Rural Community Affected by Industrial Relations Conflict." *South African Journal of Psychology,* 31 no. 4 (2001): 62–71.

Haggman, Sonia, Christopher G. Maher and Kathryn M. Refshauge. "Screening for Symptoms of Depression by Physical Therapists Managing Low Back Pain." *Journal of Physical Therapy,* 84 no. 12 (2004): 1157–1166.

Hamilton, M. "Development of a Rating Scale for Primary Depressive Illness." *British Journal of Social and Clinical Psychology,* 6 (1967): 278–296.

Jones-Webb, R. J., and L. R. Snowden. Symptoms of Depression among Blacks and Whites. *American Journal of Public Health*, 83 no. 2 (1993): 240–244.

Kabau, R., M. A. Safran, M. A. Zack, D. G. Moriarty and D. Chapman. "Sad, Blue and Depressed Days, Health Behaviours and Health Related Quality of Life, Behavioural Risk Factor Surveillance System. *Health and Quality of Life Outcomes*, 2 (2004): 40–51.

Kane, A. and M. J. Lowis. "Seasonal Affective Disorder." *South African Journal of Psychology*, 29 no. 3 (1999): 124–127.

Kockler, M., and R. Heun. "Gender Differences of Depressive Symptoms in Depressed and Non-Depressed Elderly Persons." *Internal Journal of Geriatric Psychiatry*, 17 (2002): 65–72.

Lund, C., and L. Swartz. "Xhosa-Speaking Schizophrenic Patients' Experience of Their Condition: Psychosis and *Amafufunyana.*" *South African Journal of Psychology*, 28 no. 2 (1998): 62–70.

Maciejewski, P. K., H. G. Prigerson and C. M. Mazure. "Self-Efficacy as a Mediator between Stressful Life Events and Depressive Symptoms." *British Journal of Psychiatry*, 176 (2000): 373–378.

Mazure, C. M., G. J. Longhurst and E. L. Weis. "Childhood Sexual Abuse as a Risk Factor for Adult Depression in Women: Psychosocial and Neurological Correlates." *American Journal of Psychiatry*, 156 (1999): 816–828.

Mazure, C. M., M. L. Bruce, P. K. Maciejewski and S.C. Jacobs. "Adverse Life Events and Cognitive-Personality Characteristics in the Prediction of Major Depression and Antidepressive Response. *American Journal of Psychiatry*, 157 (2000): 896–903.

McKilay, J. B., S. M. McKinlay and D. Brambilla. "The Relative Contributions of Endocrine Changes and Social Circumstances to Depression in Middle-Aged Women. *Journal of Health and Social Behaviour*, 28 (1987): 345–363.

Miller, M. C. "Women and Depression." *Harvard Mental Health Letter.* 20, (2004): 1–4.

Miroesky, J. "Age and Gender Gap in Depression." *Journal of Health and Social Behaviour*, 37 (1996): 362–380.

Miza, I., and R. Jenkins. "Risk Factors, Prevalence and Treatment of Anxiety and Depressive Disorders in Pakistan: Systemic Review. *British Medical Journal*, 328 (2004): 794–800.

Mkhize, D., and T. V. Mayekiso. "The Prevalence of Depression amongst Adolescents in the Transkei." Paper presented at the 9th National Congress of the South African Association of Child and Adolescent Psychiatry, Cape Town, South Africa, 1993.

Nolen-Hoeksema, S., and G. P. Keita. "Women and Depression." *Psychology of Women Quarterly*, 27 (2003): 89–90.

Ngubane, H. *Body and Mind in Zulu Medicine: An Ethnography of Health and Disease in Nyuswa-Zulu Thought and Practice.* London, England: Academic Press, 1977.

Oosthuizen, G. C. *Religion Alive: Studies in the New Movements and the Indigenous Church in Southern Africa.* Johannesburg, South Africa: Hodder & Stoughton, 1986.

Piccinelli, P., and G. Wilkinson. "Gender Differences in Depression." *British Journal of Psychiatry,* 177 (2000): 486–492.

Pillay, B. J. "A Model of Help Seeking Behaviour for Urban Africans." *South African Journal of Psychology*, 26 no. 1 (1996): 4–9.

Pillay, A. L., P. Naidoo and M. R. Lockhart. "Psychopathology in Urban and Rural/Peri-Urban Children Seeking Mental Health Care." *South African Journal of Psychology*, 29 no. 4 (1999): 178–183.

Pillay, Basil J., and M. H. Cassimjee. "Anxiety and Depression in an Urban General Practice." *Journal of Anxiety and Depression*, 3 no. 2 (2000): 4–5.

Rapmund, V., and C. Moore. "Women's Stories of Depression: A Constructivist Approach. *South African Journal of Psychology*, 30 no. 2 (2000): 20–30.

Robertson, A., S. Allwood and L. Giagiano. *Textbook of Psychiatry for Southern Africa.* Cape Town, South Africa: Oxford, 2003.

South African Anxiety and Depression Group. "Depression in Black South Africans." Retrieved 3 May 2006 from http://www.sadag.co.za/

Strebel, A., N. Msomi and M. Stacey. "A Gender and Racial Epidemiological Profile of Public Psychiatric Hospitals in the Western Cape." *South African Journal of Psychology*, 29 no. 2 (1999): 53–61.

Swartz, S. *Culture and Mental Health: A Southern African View.* Cape Town, South Africa: Oxford, 1998.

Wessels, W. H. "Healing within the African Context." *Psychiatric Insight*, 4 no. 3 (1987a): 34.

—. "New Developments in African Healing Practices." *Psychiatric Insight*, 4 no. 3 (1987b): 35.

Zung, W. W. "A Self-Rating Depression Scale." *Archives of General Psychiatry*, 12 (1965): 63–70.

FORCED MUSLIM RELIGIOUS SECLUSION AND VEILING FOR WOMEN AND DEPRESSION

IFFAT HUSSAIN

One of the major misconceptions about Islam is the practice of veiling (covering the face, head or the whole body with an over-garment), and the seclusion of women. The Muslim fundamentalists preached these concepts and propagated the powerlessness and vulnerability of Muslim women. The main purpose of veiling and seclusion is to prohibit mixing of men and women, which may result in sexual temptation; and it is solely the women's responsibility to avert any male attention.

Types of Veils and Seclusion

There are different concepts for maintaining seclusion and veiling. It also differs from one region of Muslim state to another. Some of the clothing or other means used are:

- Scarf – Muslim women wear scarves on their heads to cover their hair. It is believed that women should not let their hair be seen because it entices or attracts men.
- Over-garment – Some people believe that it is women's bodies which entice men, so women are forced to wear a loose over-garment to hide their figures.
- Chaddar – A big piece of cloth used to cover the head and the upper part of the body; in some cases face below eyes is also covered.
- Hijab – A veil to cover the face. Some people think it is the face that attracts men, so women should cover their faces.
- Niqab – A veil covering the lower face up to the eyes. It covers the face and shoulders completely.
- Burqa – There are two types of Burqas. One is a cloak, usually black, that covers the body from head to toe, with a light cloth over the face to see through. It is not colourful or printed, because could attract men. The second type is a black or white

cloak covering the body from head to toe but with two small holes or a mesh for the eyes.

- Four Walls – Some people believe that women's place is in home, so they are a kind of prisoner in their own houses, not allowed to go out unless it is extremely important.

An Abaya is also a long black cloak with arm slits, is worn in Persian Gulf countries. Iranian and some Lebanese women wear the "chador", a large square of fabric worn over the head and pinned under the chin. In some parts of the Gulf States, women cover their hands with long gloves. Jordanian and Syrian women generally wear scarves and loose-fitting clothes, perhaps covered by long coat. For the eyes, netting is used. In countries like Saudi Arabia, women are segregated from the world by more than dress—they are not allowed to travel alone but must be accompanied by a male relative. They are only allowed to remove their veils to eat in a restaurant if they are in an isolated cubicle with family members. They live in a very restricted environment. In more moderate countries like Egypt and Morocco, a simple head covering is used as veil. The most extreme form of veiling is the Afghan Hijab, where women wear suffocating Burqas, a shapeless form that covers the body from head to toe, with a type of face mask covering the eyes; a small grille lies over their eyes to see through. These are also worn in some regions of Pakistan along its border with Afghanistan.

These women walking in the streets are one of the most hideous sights one can witness. The major reasons for this segregation are to isolate women from the outside world and restrict their mobility, so that they are under the complete control of and dependent on men—and most of all, to restrict what is perceived as their sexual activities. They are not allowed to speak, look or associate with men. This leads to a tremendous lack of self-confidence, depression and feelings of self-pity. In some rural parts of Pakistan, Purdah (the common name for the segregation of Muslim women in Pakistan) is so strict that they are not even allowed to visit the outer rooms, verandas or gardens. These rooms are in the backyard. Male servants cannot work in their presence. These women are only allowed to see their sons, brothers, fathers, uncles and husbands. The origin of segregation lies in the deep-rooted suspicion of sexual appetites, and the purpose is to check it.

The History of the Veil

The history of the veil shows that it was used even before Islam rose to power in the Middle East. It was first the badge of identification of the wealthy upper-class women who were in the king's harem; the practice was later accepted by the followers of Prophet Mohammed because it was a sign of wealth and position. The history also shows that these were pre-Islamic practices which were later re-introduced as Islamic law. When the prophet Mohammed introduced equality for women in all fields of life, men found they were losing their monopoly and raised their voices against this, pressuring women to stick to veiling and seclusion.

Those women who have a choice whether to adopt this practice usually do so to show their devotion to Islam and the Prophet Mohammed. But in most Islamic countries the veil is considered obligatory for Muslim women, and their faith, purity and adherence to Islam is judged by their veil and seclusion. This forcible restriction has many negative physical and emotional effects on the women.

Psychological Effects and Depression in Women Due to Forced Veiling

The adverse physical effects on women who are covered with long dresses from head to toe are many. When imposed on young girls it hinders them from playing, jumping, running and most physical activities. They lose their interest in playing because it is no longer fun for them to run around in heavy long clothing, sweating under scarves. These girls do not get the exercise necessary for growing children to do in order to build their body structures, resulting in premature weariness and aging. Girls in Islamic society, particularly in strict traditional Muslim families, are brought up in a way that they know clearly their position in their family and in society. They are taught at a very young age that they are inferior, powerless and incompetent, that they must obey their male guardians, and above all they must keep their beauty hidden until they are legally married to a man. For these reasons young girls are forced to wear the Islamic veil. This not only conveys the required message but is also very effective in hindering physical movement, thus "naturally" calming them down.

When comparing young girls and women who wear veils and are brought up in strict Islamist families with those who are brought up in free environment or less Islamist families who have never worn veils, there is a great difference in their behaviour, attitudes and confidence.

Those coming from strict Islamic families and culture are very modest, soft-spoken, quiet, and have less confidence and self-esteem. They avoid eye contact, particularly with men. They usually gaze at the ground as they talk. They sit in the corners of trains and public areas, usually looking out of the windows and watching on the ground or their own feet. These young girls and women try to walk in groups. They are constantly worried and scared of their surroundings. They are encouraged and prefer to stay indoors as much as possible, and therefore are less experienced in their social lives. For this reason they depend on their male family members to do most of the outdoor business for them.

Under the pressure of being caged inside moving prisons, these adult women grow depressed and unnerved. They are also taught that Islam discourages them to laugh loudly, to dance in public, to listen to music or sing, because these acts may arouse men's feelings towards them and make them commit a sin. Then the responsibility for this is on women's shoulders.

Laughing, playing, music and dancing are all elements of happiness and cheerful life. As these women are forbidden these elements and restrictions are imposed on them, their lives are dull, depressed and gloomy. These women are not seen at parties; mostly they gather in mourning ceremonies. Therefore most of the mourning ceremonies are full of these women who are looking for a place to gather around and cry their problems out.

These women do not enjoy styling their hair, using make-up and wearing fashionable clothes. If they must do so, it should be hidden under their veils, so as not to display their beauty. Veils hide their beauty and make them unattractive to men, which in turn increases their worthless and lowers their self-esteem. These women are then emotionally and physically separated from the world around them. With this they experience loneliness, depression and frustration. Their feelings of worthlessness and of being unneeded in this world, the constant humiliation and the burden of being responsible for arousing males' sinful attraction towards them, makes them very timid and helpless individuals. It is made clear to them from the beginning that their dangerous female bodies can be the main cause of fornication if they are not careful to cover themselves.

When they don't see a way out of their prison, these women drown into deep depression and commit suicide. One of the very popular acts of suicide is described by the Iranian Pervin Darabi in *Rage against the Veil*, where she describes the suicidal act against veil of her sister, the Iranian political activist and medical doctor Homa Darabi.

Homa Darabi was a respected female child psychiatrist in both Iran and USA. She committed one of the most painful and most shocking forms of suicide: public self-immolation. She removed her scarf from her head (in Iran she could have arrested and beaten for such behaviour and sent to prison for one year) and wandered through crowds of people shouting "death to tyranny! Long live freedom!" Several people pleaded her to stop and to cover her head; she didn't. The she removed her coat, soaked the lower part of her body with gasoline and ignited a match. She was immediately engulfed in flames. For few seconds she remained on her feet and then she collapsed on the ground. Tears poured from her eyes and she continued to cry out.

Pervin explains that Homa was appalled by the laws of Veiling and Seclusion. She always spoke to her on the telephone, telling of her mounting horror, how women are tortured and about public stoning executions of women who, intentionally or not, broke the laws of strict Islamic appearance and conduct. Homa lost her teaching appointments and private practice because she refused to fully comply with the mandatory rules of Veiling. She slipped into the dark world of depression and hopelessness, and publicly committed suicide.

There are Muslim fundamentalists and extremists who misinterpret Quran verses and use them as laws. In this way they manage to brainwash people. According to these fundamentalists, Allah does not want to see women outside their homes, they are created to stay home for the purpose of household jobs, and it is a sin if they go out of their homes. They assert that the Islamic faith denies women the right to express or enjoy their own sexuality. These fundamentalists have also brainwashed Muslims believing that women are inherently evil and the majority of the occupants of hell are women, so women must be very modest and careful not to commit any sin at all. This veiling is designed to protect the dignity of women, and they must cover themselves from strangers outside of the family. They must cover their faces and heads and wear an over-garment when they go outside their homes.

> A Turkish (Dutch) father allows his sons to go out as often as he likes, but he forbids his daughter to do the same. The father does this because of the fact that girls run more risks and are more vulnerable and because he finds it good and right that, boys have more freedom than girls. (Verkuyten & Slooter, 2007: 471)

But many Muslims apologists argue that head and face covering for Muslim women is not mandated in the Quran, and the Quran does not suggest that women should be veiled or they should be kept apart from the world of men. They have the right to decide what is appropriate for them, and the Quran is insistent on the full participation of women in society and in the religious practices prescribed for men. They also argue that Islam liberated women more than 1,400 hundred years ago. Mernissi argues that veil is used to punish Muslim women, making them timid and mutilated companions:

> How did Islamic traditions succeed in transforming the Muslim women into that submissive, marginal creature who buries herself and only goes out into the world timidly and huddled in their veils? Why do the Muslim men need such a mutilated companion? (Mernissi, 1991: 194)

> Fadela Amara, the cities minister, who is of Algerian origin, says the Burqa is a prison. "It is not a religious sign but the visible sign of a totalitarian political project preaching sexual inequality," she said. (Economist, 2008: 72)

But Muslim fundamentalists have done tremendous work to brainwash men as well as women concerning women's segregation. Many women blame themselves for not observing segregation and working along with men. They stated that they feel depressed when they think about this because they believe that Allah will punish them for not observing segregation. A forty-three year old woman working in a chemical laboratory said:

> Allah recommends that we should wear a veil when we are among strangers, and this elevates women's honour and respect. I don't wear any type of veil because it is not permitted at my work. My manager and supervisor do not permit it. Since I work in chemical laboratory they say it is dangerous, because we have to work with chemicals and fire. I feel guilty for not wearing it because there are so many boys and men as well who work in this lab. I know I am committing a sin, but Allah knows that I have no choice. I have to do this job because I need the money. I hope he will forgive.

Another woman, twenty-seven years old and working in computer sales said:

> I feel very bad for not veiling and maintaining seclusion. It is our religious duty. But I show my face in public and at work place which is very un-Islamic. I am working not because I need the money, but to keep myself busy and to use my education. I know I am doing wrong. I should stay home. But at home it is very boring. My colleagues also tell me to continue

until I get married. I feel guilty for not maintaining seclusion or veiling myself. It is not accepted in the office so I can't wear it.

Some said that they have to cover their heads and faces to make Allah happy, but it depresses them. They feel lonely and lag behind socially.

A woman about twenty-nine years of age who works in the telesales department of a national company and wears a veil said:

There are girls who always come to the office wearing beautiful clothes in the latest fashions. They also wear make-up and matched jewellery. They think too highly of themselves and ignore me like I am nobody. There are three of us girls who wear chaddars in the office. They treat us as if we are lower-class, backward and conservative.

In describing the class struggle between the old elite (the white Turks) and a new ruling class, Turgut says in her article "Veiled Hostility":

At an upscale shopping mall in Istanbul last week, I heard a group of teenage girls with big hair and designer jeans proclaim loudly as two head-scarved young women approached: "Why do they have to come here? Can't they go somewhere else?" Some university professors have declared that they won't teach head-scarved students, while Deniz Baykal, leader of the opposition Republican People's Party, speaks of the head scarf in militaristic terms as "uniforms imposed by outside forces." (Turgut, 2008: 14)

Such remarks these by teenage girls and behaviour of university professors towards these women who are forced to wear head scarves increases the inferiority complexes of these women, adding to the feelings of worthlessness and of not belonging to this world.

Duplaix, who worked as a teacher with North African and Jewish students explains in her article "Yes" about an incident when three sixteen-year-old girls started to wear Islamic scarves under the influence of a male Moroccan classmate:

The young girls who put on their head scarves before leaving the building tell me privately that they are a means of protection. Without them, they say, some people would consider them "easy" and they would be "prey to insults". (Duplaix, 2004: 36)

The face- and head-covering shows the inequality and inferior status of women. Girls are taught at an early age to accept their lower status and to maintain segregation as soon as they start school. This is related to their dignity and family's honour: as a result they become scared and timid.

A twenty-three-year-old woman who works for a multinational company described the helplessness of a co-worker who observes seclusion in her own way:

> I think to wear a veil and work with men are two different things. I have one colleague who wears a big chaddar. She sits in the corner most of the time and does her work. She doesn't like to socialise with others, maybe because she is very timid and helpless. If we ask her to sit with us for lunch or tea, she does, but she sits there so quietly, as if she is alone. She is just few years older than me, I guess, but she does not enjoy the jokes we do and has no fun in life. I feel sorry for her.

There are women who speak against the practice of seclusion and veiling:

> I don't understand that why men are so free, and women have to avoid even their gaze. Men are ordered by Islamic law to lower their gaze around women, so why is there so much fuss about women's dress and veiling? Why not ask men to lower their gazes and not look at women who are strangers? Men will also be judged by God for what they did in this life—it is not only women who will be asked what they did in this world.

> Some authors explain that the male-Islamic clergy described the veil as a symbol of the Muslim women's obedience to Islamic principles, and all good Muslim women should engage themselves in this practice. (Siddiqi, 1983; Afshar, 1985; Philips & Jones, 1985; Al-Swailem, 1995).

These clergymen use series of passages from the Quran such as "not to display their beauty and ornaments" and "draw their head cover over their bosoms and not display their ornaments" (S.24:31) to support these practices. They also argue that the male sexuality is ignited and aroused when men come into social contact with women: therefore pious Islamic women should veil themselves so as not to arouse men's sexuality. The purpose of the veil is to check this social contact and protect women's virtue and piousness and safeguard them from lustful eyes (Siddiqi, 1983: viii; Philips & Jones, 1985: 39–46; Al-Swailem, 1995: 27–29).

Symptoms and Complaints of Veiled and Secluded Women

The women who are forced into segregation or are brainwashed to do it always lag behind in social, physical and mental activities. These women lack perceived life control. They are very submissive, cannot make personal decisions and feel that they have no personal power over themselves. They do not get the social or emotional support they require. They are very dependent on their friends, family and relatives. Most of these women derive their identities, their sense of self from being a wife or a mother. Even culturally this is accepted and considered honourable for these women. They are dependent on others in all aspects of life, including their financial support. They accomplish very little, because they are taught and made fully conscious by their environment that they are lower than men and must be obedient and submissive: "The social role has a complex effect on their psychological well-being" (Miller, 1998: 371). According to Betz (1993), the secluded homemaker women who do not have other outlets for achievements and productivity are highly susceptible to psychological distress. The least satisfied with their lives were those who'd been housewives all their lives.

> Both greater exposure to stressful life events and lack of access to coping resources (personal, social and economic), appear to contribute to women's excess in depression. (McGrath et al., 1990, quoted in Betz, 1993: 393)

"Women are being discriminated against because of culture and race which are primary stressor in their lives." (Majumdar, 1998: 51).

It is a cultural and religious belief that women are by nature inferior to men. They are trained to believe that family responsibilities are more important for women than their personal careers. Even highly educated girls are trained to be submissive and taught the twin virtues of patience and sacrifice. The veil is not just a dress code: it is a specific kind of behaviour, an expression of what society expects of them. It determines women's psychology, social and physical development and determines the way they speak, walk, look or even social contact and mixing with other people.

> She represents a deficiency compared to the man; it is expected of her that she takes up a complementary, subordinate position in relation to the man. (Gressgard, 2006: 325)

These segregated women tend to complain of vague and diffuse symptoms, focusing on somatic complaints such as pain and weakness, and often connected to one particular bodily organ, the heart. "Insufficient social support should be considered an important risk factor for ill-health and mortality" (Fuhrer, 1999: 77). "Women are two to three times more likely than men to experience depression in their life time." (McGrath et al., 1990, quoted in Matlin, 1993: 447).

> Poverty, domestic isolation, powerlessness and patriarchal oppression, are all associated with higher prevalence of psychiatric morbidity in women. (Desjarlais, 1995: 183)

Most of the segregated women show at least three to four of the following signs and symptoms, if not more:

- Weight gain
- Loss of interest and pleasure in activities
- Persistent sad and empty moods
- Feelings of hopelessness and pessimism
- Irritability, anger and frustration
- Low levels of energy and constant fatigue
- Feelings of worthlessness
- Feelings of inappropriate guilt
- Inability to concentrate
- Inability to make decisions
- Constant feelings of sadness and grief
- Physical symptoms such as headaches, digestive disorders and chronic pain.

In addition to all these symptoms, such restrictions of head and face covering and/or complete segregation results in ignorance, superstition, obesity, anaemia and premature aging of Muslim women. Muslim women are almost always segregated from their male family members at Islamic functions, as well as in other social functions. Some mosques have solid partitions so that they can be visually and audibly isolated. Some men also discourage their women from going to mosques, because in most cases there is hardly any space for women. Women must pray in their own homes.

While going through the process of mandatory and forced veiling/ seclusion, these young women go through various psychological traumas. They are deprived of mental and moral nourishment; because they are deprived of a healthy social life and segregated from the outer world, they engage their minds in petty family quarrels, with the result that they become narrow and restricted in their outlook. They lag behind, cannot take part in outdoor activities, and are weighed down by a slavish mentality and an inferiority complex. They have no desire for knowledge, because they are taught not to be interested in anything outside the four walls of the house. Seclusion also has its deteriorating effects upon the physical constitution of Muslim women. They are usually victims of anaemia, tuberculosis and pyorrhea. Their bodies are deformed, with bent backs and drooping shoulders. Their joints and bones hurt due to lack of physical activities from childhood. They very often develop heart palpitations. The result of all this is severe depression and ultimately early death.

These women are brainwashed to believe that if they will not observe seclusion and veiling they will go to hell. So by covering their faces and hair and wearing an over-garment they believe that they are earning their places in heaven. Some of the young girls said that it gives them moral support and comfort for what they want to achieve—a place in heaven. And this veiling gives a big "No" signal to them and to others: by "no", they mean a stop to sexual desire. Some women are confused. In reality they don't want to wear the veil, but because they think it is an order from God they do it, believing that if they disobey they will not go to heaven. They feel very helpless and uncomfortable in this matter. "The veiled women link the veil to men's desires to control women and unwillingness to manage their own sexuality" (Bartkowski & Read, 2003: 83). Bartkowski and Read quoted further comments from unveiled Muslim women:

> Their accounts often reiterate Islamic feminist arguments that the veil is used as a patriarchal tool of oppression imposed on Muslim women. (Ibid)

Discussion and Conclusions

It is a depressing life for these Muslim women who are forced into seclusion and veiling. Deep down in their hearts they do not like it, but they will be blamed and to made feel ashamed if they will try to get rid of it or go out without covering themselves. The brainwashers have done superb work of putting fear into these unfortunate women: they fear going to hell if they disobey, they fear being shunned by the society, they fear being alone, they fear losing financial security, they lack self-confidence and therefore cannot break the hold their husbands have over them. It is very common in the summer to see a Muslim women covered from head to toe with an over-garment while her husband is next to her only in shorts. And this double standard is always defended with great ease—it is God's order for women. This is clearly a sexiest attitude. Imposing the veil on women is the ultimate proof that men do not trust women with their faces and bodies. Some of these men who are perturbed at the sight of a Muslim woman's hair or neck have no problem freely mixing with non-Muslim women, greeting them with hugs or shaking hands. This duplicity is always overlooked. This mentality must be exposed and challenged.

While modesty is a religious prescription, the covering of faces and hair and seclusion are not religious requirements of Islam: these restrictions were introduced by fundamentalists. They dictate it as a necessary part of Muslim women's attire, as a part of the Islamic dress. These women in particular become helpless, timid and unfit for any fight in life. The Muslim world has managed to suppress half of its population—women—by using this means to oppress and prevent them from developing their full human potential.

Considering the large number of veiled women in Islamic states, one can easily understand the vastness and seriousness of the problem of veiling and seclusion. There are serious misunderstandings among scholars and layman alike concerning the issue, and it requires re-examination and re-interpretation. Muslim women need moral guidance to show them that they can be modest and virtuous without the help of veils and seclusion—that they do not have to cover their heads and faces and to wear an over-garment to be good. They can be respected for what they achieve in life and how they use their brains, and most of all as human beings. Difficult and challenging as it may be to do so, the issue of veiling and seclusion as defined by Islamic society requires that we should take a careful, considered look at the multilayered complexity of these women's lives and of their relationship to the practices of veiling and seclusion. We also need to examine the issue from a host of women's life experiences and view points, and guide them accordingly.

These forcibly secluded women do not have a feeling of personal power and control over what happens to them, and they know that they will not get social and emotional support if they go against it. They lack perceived life control and social and emotional support. Thus their sense of self-worth is clearly related to their psychological health. They are in pain and in need of help. The only way out of this dark prison of depression for these women is the withdrawal of political Islamic laws, and the end of this practice used to control women in the name of Islam.

Bibliography

Afshar, H. "The Legal, Social and Political Position of Women in Iran." *International Journal of the Sociology of Law*, 13 (1989): 47–60.

Al-Swailem, A. A. "Introduction." In H. Abdullah, *A Comparison Between Veiling and Unveiling*. Riyadh, Saudi Arabia: Dar-us-Salaam Publications, 1995.

Bartkowski, J. P., and J. G. Read. "Veiled Submission: Gender, Power and Identity among Evangelical and Muslim Women in the United States." *Qualitative Sociology*, 26 no.1 (Spring 2003):71–92.

Betz, N. 1993. "Women's Career Development." In F. L. Denmark and M. A. Paludi, eds., *Psychology of Women: A Handbook of Issues and Theories*. Westport, CT: Greenwood Press.

Chanen, J. S. "Practicing on Faith." *ABA Journal*, 94 no. 3 (2008): 11.

Darabi, P. *Rage against the Veil*. New York, NY: Prometheus Books, 2000.

Duplaix, T. "Yes." *Time Canada*, 163 no. 6 (2004): 36–37.

Fuhrer, R., S. A. Stansfeld, J. Chemali and M. J. Shipley. "Gender, Social Relations and Mental Health: Prospective Findings from an Occupational Cohort (Whitehall II study)." *Social Science and Medicine* 48 (1993): 77–87.

Gressgard, R. "The Veiled Muslim, the Anorexic and the Transsexual: What Do They Have in Common?" *European Journal of Women Studies*, 13 no. 4 (2006): 325.

Guindi, F. E. *Veil: Modesty, Privacy and Resistance*. Oxford, England: Berg Publishers, 1999.

Hawkins, S. "The Essence of the Veil: The Veil as a Metaphor of Islamic Women." *Journal of Biblical Manhood and Womanhood*, Spring (2004): 29–34.

Hussain, I. *Problems of Working Women in Karachi, Pakistan*. Newcastle upon Tyne, England: Cambridge Scholars Publishing, 2008.

Majumdar, B., and S. Ladak. "Management of Family and Workplace Stress Experienced by Women of Colour from Various Cultural Backgrounds." *Canadian Journal of Public Health*. 89 no.1 (1998): 48–52.

Matlin, M. W. *The Psychology of Women*. Belmont, CA: Wadsworth Publishing, 2003.

Mernissi, F. *The Veil and the Male Elite: A Feminist Interpretation of Women's Rights in Islam*. New York, NY: Addison-Wesley Publishing, 1991.

Miller, A. M., J. E. Wilbur, A. C. Montgomery and P. Chandler. "Social Role Quality and Psychology Well Being." *AAOHN Journal*, 46 no. 8 (1998): 371–78.

Philips, A. A. B., and J. Jones. *Polygamy in Islam*. Riyadh, Saudi Arabia: International Islamic Publishing: 1985.

Siddiqui, M. I. *Islam Forbids Free Mixing of Men and Women*. Lahore, Pakistan: Kazi, 1983.

Turget, P. "Veiled Hostility." *Time Canada*, 171 no. 9 (2008): 14–15.

Verkuyten, M., and L. Slooter. "Tolerance of Muslim Beliefs and Practices: Age-Related Differences and Context Effects." *International Journal of Behavioural Development* 31 (2007): 467–477.

Werbner, Pnina. "Veiled Interventions in Pure Space—Honour, Shame and Embodied Struggles among Muslims in Britain and France." *Theory, Culture and Society*, 24 no. 2 (2007): 161–186.

—. "A Burqa Barrier." *The Economist*, 387 no. 8589 (2008): 61.

—. "Covering Up." *The Economist*, 387 no. 8582 (2008): 56.

—. "Veils of Half Truth." *The Economist*, 386 no. 8567 (2008). 58–59.

MULTIPLE LOSS AND GRIEF, WITH UNDERLYING FACTORS— A CASE STUDY

BELINDA CODY

Introduction

This is a case study describing the therapeutic strategies undertaken by an adult female client in response to profound and complex loss which had lead to depression. This period of her life involved the deaths of several close loved ones, and the intergenerational impact of the revelation of concealed and confusing family origins. These events all took place within a period of just over a year. The client, whom we shall call Sophia, was a recently trained counsellor. She consulted me for Creative Arts Therapy sessions for a period of about eighteen months but also drew on the expertise of a GP, a teacher of improvised music, and a psychologist. The focus of this article will be the efficacy of recovery strategies involving a multi-disciplinary network of therapeutic specialists.

Sophia presented as a resourceful individual who felt she had enough knowledge, training, and life experience to get through a period of grief with sadness, certainly, but also considerable optimism. In addition, she was of the opinion that she was a strong person, as she had successfully overcome many difficult challenges in the past. Furthermore, Sophia was a highly qualified counsellor. However, she was not prepared for the added impact of multiple deaths within a short period, nor was she prepared for the further impact that arose as these losses coincided with revelations regarding her father's previously unknown origins, which compounded and complicated the losses, and eventually resulted in a decline in her health together with an unexpected period of depression. I briefly outline the various strategies, from both the medical and complementary health models, that the client employed to help her successfully navigate this complex period in a meaningful way.

Background

When Sophia's mother, living some distance away in a country town, was diagnosed with cancer and given six months to live, my client, then a single parent, took on the role of full-time carer. She was driving considerable distances every week until her mother's death, as her own children still needed regular care and support.

In the early months, Sophia experienced enormous anticipatory grief for her mother's actual and impending losses, while organising the Palliative Care team, her mother's medications, regular hospital visits for chemotherapy, and her mother's home and garden. Sophia had just set out to establish her own private practice but it was not possible to proceed under the circumstances, and this activity had to be put on hold indefinitely, resulting in a considerable loss of income and independence.

Some weeks later, on a brief return visit home, the client learned of the shocking suicide of a very close creative friend. The friend's suicide was precipitated by depression. Following this traumatic and extremely distressing loss, enormous grief and loss engulfed her whole community. Sophia experienced further grief, loss, bewilderment, and a feeling of social disintegration, while still caring for her dying mother. She received little acknowledgement of this loss from members of her family. She was still caring for her terminally ill mother, including care of her house and garden, as other siblings were unavailable due to distance or other care demands. So there was no time, or context, to properly mourn this traumatic loss.

Sophia's mother then suffered a serious physical injury during her treatment while under overnight respite care, resulting in further pain, loss of mobility, dignity, independence, and opportunity for her, in addition to her terminal illness, and further complexities for Sophia as her carer.

At this time, Sophia received the first revelations of her father's previously concealed origins and heritage, bringing shock and disbelief. While she had long intuited that earlier information about her father's lineage was untrue, she was not at all prepared for the actuality, the circumstances, or the characters involved in the new revelations. Her mother denied any knowledge of the new information.

With important family and friends leaving to live overseas, Sophia reported beginning to experience a serious loss of support and closeness, and growing feelings of isolation. Sophia's mother died in her own home, six months after the initial diagnosis. Sophia was with her for her dying, which she experienced as a deep sadness, but also a great privilege. However, further complications then arose involving her family responsibilities, while Sophia received little support. This also left no time to properly grieve this death either. This was an extremely complex period, and Sophia had little time to process events to date or to function effectively, as she had little energy available to deal with the recent bereavements and no time for reflection.

Manifestations of early depression began to make it difficult for Sophia to function fully or to comfortably deal with duties and activities on a daily basis, with ensuing loss of contact with friends, hardship for her own family, erosion of broader family understanding and relationships, and incapacity to engage in more than a minimal amount of work. In addition to rising debt and immense grief, she experienced chronic health problems such as acute anxiety, breathlessness, and chronic exhaustion. Other major health problems included chronic bronchitis and severe sinusitis, skin conditions, imminent organ malfunction, incapacity to concentrate or think under pressure, serious cognitive impairment, seriously eroded capacity to plan for the future, panic attacks, and deepening dissociation and dislocation. Sophia began to realise that she was becoming increasingly disabled and experienced a growing sense of isolation. Furthermore, owing to the actual and secretive nature of her father's background, there never had been extended family members available for support. Up until this point, Sophia thought she had been coping well. She had not registered that she was actually becoming depressed, as she was feeling too overwhelmed initially, and too emotionally numbed to recognise the signs of the emerging condition.

She eventually became aware of developing depression, leading to a state focused on recent losses, the past, and, in this vulnerable condition, the intrusion of previous traumatic events from her early life.

Underlying Factors

Her grieving was further compounded throughout this period by the discovery of her father's true origins and heritage. However, it was not until after her mother's funeral that she found herself grieving his losses throughout his life, and those that resulted for her and the family. The information precipitated a serious health crisis for her, especially around the revelation that other close family members had been living in proximity throughout her upbringing, but had never overtly acknowledged the existence of the family connection (as most of them had no knowledge of the facts, either). Her father's dreams and rightful opportunities for a better life were effectively thwarted by the past, by a family story that was concealed from him and lack of acknowledgement. Thus Sophia was increasingly burdened with the realisation of her father's life-long but un-revealed loneliness, powerlessness, and social isolation arising from a lack of family links, and support for himself and his children in the absence and denial of a loving family network.

Sophia was managing reasonably well under the circumstances following the deaths and losses, but recovery became more complex as she reflected on the traumatic news and the implications of her father's long-concealed background. She was particularly aware of the fact that the family had been denied loving contact, and had no knowledge of their rightful cultural heritage as a direct result of the concealment; therefore they had no cultural compass and no network of intimate links in their community or beyond. She began to trace later difficulties in her own life and in the lives of her siblings back to this absence and denial in their early experience.

As Sophia was in an already vulnerable state, this particular factor seems to have greatly undermined her capacity for dealing comfortably with other events at the time, and the resulting stresses began to impact on her immune system; complicating mental and physical health problems ensued, and several further losses were immediately ahead.

After having received verification of his origins from within a deeply marginalised and stigmatised group, Sophia's father, still in his fifties, then kept his own terminal illness, twenty years earlier, from the family. Sophia came to believe that her father's sudden death was a direct response to learning, too late of his family's existence and the real nature of his heritage. This knowledge had always been denied to him, and apparently he could not bring himself to share the news with even his most intimate family members, even knowing he was dying. A brief private funeral had been held for him following his unexpected and unexplained death twenty years before, with only immediate family present, reflecting the social isolation that had been forced on the family unit.

Once Sophia learned of her father's origins she began to experience enormous grief, felt even more intensely than at the time of his death, as by now she was aware of the intergenerational impact of the withholding of his real origins—and how deeply it had affected him, his children, and even his grandchildren. She expressed that she experienced the impact as immense, interconnecting with painful losses from the past together with the recent losses, and that it carried intergenerational repercussions into the future.

Further Losses

A series of other unexpected losses followed soon after. A friend became very ill, but Sophia had no energy to support her. Supportive neighbours moved away around that time, and her isolation deepened. Then Sophia had the task of selling the family home with the rest of her family absent; she was under stress to get an acceptable price in order to maximise the inheritance of all beneficiaries. She was responsible for the care of the family home up until the settlement date after the sale, which involved continued long-distance driving to the country and the necessary manual work. She reported that she found the actual process of selling deeply distressing and emotionally painful.

The eventual sale of her mother's home meant the loss of the family residence of almost fifty years, with the resultant sense of dislocation and significant additional losses, including those of the sole family cultural site, the significant place of shared history, and the indelible location of childhood memory. It took nearly a year to achieve a successful sale. Sophia experienced a lack of acknowledgement and caring from others around this loss, and enormous pressure to sell for maximum return. Also, as the eldest, she appeared to have the strongest attachment to the sense of history that the house represented and the stories it held (both told and untold), so she felt the loss most acutely. By this time, Sophia was feeling traumatised and exhausted, exhibiting very low energy levels.

In addition, Sophia's own family lacked her full support, as they faced major difficulties in their own lives and had to deal with the mystifying fact that their mother was now not well, unable to support them appropriately despite their needs, and that she was in fact experiencing depression with associated sensory and social disconnection.

A few months later, upon the shocking death of another dear and valued friend from a sudden incurable illness and then the death of a another family member soon after, Sophia reported that by the time of the latter she registered little emotional response. The subsequent experience of emotional numbness lead my client to realise she needed to seek professional assistance and support in order to salvage her declining health.

Strategies

Sophia sought assistance during the period from several different specialists from a range of therapeutic modalities. She initially consulted her local GP; she also drew support from the therapeutic use of the arts, with myself as her Creative Arts Therapist, in parallel with workshops in improvised music. In addition, she sought a referral to a psychologist for narrative therapy.

GP. Sophia had been consulting with her local doctor regarding emerging chronic medical problems following the loss of her friend and then her mother. She reported that her GP was very supportive, listening empathically and dealing effectively with her medical issues, but as time passed the doctor could not pinpoint reasons for her continuing poor health. Sophia was not willing to take anti-depressants, and fortunately her doctor was open to supporting other recovery strategies. But, with no real recovery in sight, and as she had not had the opportunity or consulting time to tell the doctor of underlying factors regarding the impact of her father's story, the GP began to realise that she did not have the appropriate skills to deal with the problem that seemed to be underpinning the growing list of chronic and debilitating medical conditions Sophia was presenting. Eventually, Sophia was offered a referral to see a local psychologist, and was placed on a waiting list.

Psychologist. By the time a psychologist became available, Sophia had been consulting me for about a year. At this stage she had begun to experience the need to try to express the story in a more verbal fashion, in narrative form in a safe and receptive environment, to strengthen her capacity for story-telling around her most profoundly disturbing loss—that of her father's life and heritage, and the associated losses in his life and her own.

The story was complex, but Sophia felt the need to feel more comfortable about telling fragments of the story to herself and to others. She had initially felt overwhelmed each time she attempted to tell anyone; the listeners had found it too stressful as well, so she had avoided speaking on the subject. Once she had access to this hidden story, she found the experience of revealing her family origins to others was unexpectedly painful, confusing, and alienating, rather than joyful, connecting, and affirming.

Sophia consulted with the psychologist for over six months, while informing her psychologist that she was still consulting occasionally with her Creative Arts Therapist. She gradually became more comfortable articulating the pieces of the story with the support of the psychologist, and continued to deal with very complex feelings against the background of the other losses.

As the psychotherapeutic process went on, Sophia slowly began to feel safer to tell parts of the story, and able to express details with less emotional arousal and more coherence. She was also better able to face and begin to deal with the implications of the story. She used the sessions with the psychologist to try to further understand the meaning of the story and its ramifications for the lives of her father, her birth family, herself and her children, though in a very complex narrative.

In addition, Sophia used the time to verbalise and further process her responses to each of the deaths that had occurred, and to eventually begin to make a place for each of their stories in her life with less emotional disturbance. This opportunity was available to her through the narrative therapy sessions that took place with the psychologist.

Creative Arts Therapies

Following her consultations with her GP and prior to seeing a psychologist, Sophia sought out a Creative Arts Therapist to begin expressing some of the chaotic emotions around the loss and grief she had experienced. As her Creative Arts Therapist, I saw her for several therapy session cycles within an eighteen-month timeframe.

Presentation. Sophia had valued and been involved in singing most of her life, but with the accumulation of events and demands, she soon experienced very low creative energy. She found her voice had become almost uncontrollable (as she also experienced intersections with past loss, recalling her loss of voice as a child raised in a rather violent community). Consequently, she experienced a loss of sense of self as a spirited artist and performer. Sophia persevered with her singing, but with loss of vocal control she felt she needed to express herself through a different medium at that time. She presented with very flattened affect, great sadness and anger, and chaotic nervous energy. I suggested that she explore painting in a therapeutic setting.

Painting. As her Creative Arts Therapist, I supported, listened, and encouraged Sophia to paint on a large scale. She painted in my consulting room/studio in cycles of three weeks, with occasional gaps when she needed to consult her GP for ongoing severe health problems. The work centred around sadness, anger, incredulity, and sense of immense loss regarding her father's story, in conjunction with processing the individual bereavements, the circumstances of each very different from the next. Sophia completed several cycles of Creative Arts Therapy sessions over eighteen months. She often cried while painting, and appeared very chaotic at that point in the recovery process. She seemed to be very conscious of bodily states and gestures at this time, and I observed that she preferred full body movement during the painting process. Most of the paintings were done standing, and exhibiting large bodily movements at the canvas. She was tearful and hyperventilating much of the time, but reported feeling somewhat calmer and relieved by the end of most sessions. Sophia talked sometimes, mostly about overwhelming feelings regarding fragments of her story, while grappling with what was in fact a confusing narrative in an understandably incoherent manner. The sessions ran for ninety minutes each. Sophia completed about twenty-two works on paper, large canvas, and board, in acrylics and mixed media. They were all quite abstract. She seemed especially drawn to mixed media, largely in earth tones. She often painted with her hands.

In addition, at my recommendation, and over several months, Sophia completed several small sketchbooks of non-dominant hand drawings (mostly pencil), drawn blind (without looking at the page), in her own time. We regularly discussed aspects of these drawings at the start of each session. These discussions often provided a starting point for the session. The sketchbooks seemed to offer her a very contained medium for the release and expression of (in particular) unaddressed, negative and confusing emotions. Sophia eventually completed over 250 drawings in this way, and reports that she maintained the practice beyond our consultation time, finding in this form an effective and portable, ongoing additional non-verbal medium for reflection and expression.

At our last consultation, Sophia discussed with me how she was increasingly drawn to music improvisation, which had become an additional and meaningful agent in her recovery, and an engaging way to access a new voice.

Music improvisation. Eventually, Sophia found herself drawn to music improvisation as a possible exploratory and recovery medium. She was still unable to sing satisfactorily, yet she felt the need at this point for a medium in which to find a "voice". I encouraged her attendance at these sessions as a further extension of the therapeutic arts process in which she was then engaged. At the time, Sophia was facing the most chaotic period to date, and experienced overwhelming feelings of panic and a shutting down of cognitive function when under any pressure. She began to attend regular improvised music workshops, and committed to daily sessions of up to three hours long of solo music improvisation practice. She found her senses of reliable emotional nourishment, creative freedom, aesthetic reconnection and autonomy very gradually returning. Sophia resonated with improvisation, as absence of structure previously unexplained in her early background had forced her to rely on improvisatory methods in many areas of her life. Instrumental musical improvisation became for her an increasingly accessible safe space, sometimes guided by simple parameters, including colour and imagery, in the presence of a skilled and sensitive teacher of improvised music. Initially, Sophia reported feeling quite handicapped, with greatly flattened affect, and struggled with understanding every aspect, still unable to rely on thinking, or memory, necessary for comprehending technical details. However, with support and encouragement, and keeping to the simplest of forms and sounds she could manage, Sophia proceeded slowly and became more comfortable as she was able to express herself more freely in improvised musical form.

The improvised music sessions, offered without any pressure, seemed to provide some emotional containment and a creative sensory field of experience untainted by the events and subsequent responses that had contributed to her depressed condition and accompanying poor health. Sophia seemed to benefit from emotional engagement within a sonic environment in association with whole body coordination when able to make the free choices that improvisation offered. She referred to a feeling of discovering a deep sense of original sonic resonance at this time. Improvisation also offered the client the possibility of engaging and musically communicating with other improvisers in improvised music making, a sophisticated form of non-verbal interaction. This group provided a small community of sympathetic and musically receptive others, reducing her sense of isolation.

Sophia's chronic anxiety slowly began to diminish, and there was a very gradual emergence, though with some lapses, over the next year, with slowly improving memory and thinking, the slow re-emergence of learning capacity, and the beginnings of more sustained positive health.

While Sophia eventually exhibited reduced signs of depression, she reported that she still found it somewhat unsafe to tell any but a select few of her family background to date, having already encountered blatant discrimination on several attempts. However, she also reported that she felt optimistic that she would eventually be able to put more of the pieces of the story together, as her concentration continued to improve. She began to realise that, as she became more accepting of the confusing and paradoxical nature of the story, and began to enjoy a more consistent sense of wellbeing and equilibrium brought about through her chosen therapeutic supports, she could also begin to re-establish her sense of self in the context of her new knowledge about her family origins.

Some time later, Sophia was gradually more able to work professionally once again, although not in her chosen field. She resumed some study, and was also a participant in a small improvised music community. She continued to pursue further reflective work, especially with improvised music, as her health showed increasing stability and the disabilities she experienced began gradually to recede. She reported coming to the beginnings of a more integrated health status.

Conclusion

The actual depression seemed to have lasted for about four months, though with considerable residual disability, especially in cognitive areas, for more than a year. Sophia began to report slowly returning optimism, and gradually increasing re-engagement with the world around her. This client had held a belief that she was a strong person who would never be a candidate for depression. However, her experience through this period contradicted her belief that she, even with her training, was invulnerable to depression. It was a humbling experience for her. Depression overtook her when she was doing her very best to cope with multiple deaths and deep losses, and the compromising of her health as a consequence of additional stresses related to the revelation of a disturbing family secret. Fortunately, once Sophia had recognised and accepted that she was actually depressed, she was able to actively engage in a process of seeking the necessary and appropriate professional help at each stage of her therapeutic journey.

Sophia found she needed a range of therapeutic approaches and effective alternatives to pharmaceutical options to support her as her needs changed. In light of this, Sophia showed courage in undertaking such a wholistic personal exploration while seeking assistance from a range of therapeutic modalities in order to find support and meaning through the grief and loss she was confronted with during a tumultuous chapter in mid-life.

This case study has articulated some of the benefits of a multi-disciplinary approach to therapy regarding Sophia's experiences of depression and serious health issues, especially in relation to multiple deaths and complex loss, including awareness of the significance of underlying factors such as the explosive emergence of a family secret involving chaotic and confusing inter-generational ramifications. The combination of medical, psychological, and inter-modal creative arts therapies interventions provided a network of appropriate and effective support to this client on her path towards meaningful personal renewal following a period of depression.

DEPRESSION IN FEMALE SPINAL CORD INJURED PATIENTS: THE EXPERIENCE OF LOSS

NANCY MOODLEY AND BASIL J. PILLAY

Introduction

Spinal cord injury (SCI) results in an interruption of the nerve signals from the brain to parts of the body below the injury which leads to paraplegia ("paralysis below the chest or waist and involves the trunk and lower limbs") or quadriplegia ("tetraplegia were the upper limbs are also affected") (Spinal Cord Injury Resources, n.d, 1).

> Quadriplegia occurs when there is damage to the spinal cord in the cervical region whilst paraplegia occurs when there is impairment at or below the T1 thoracic level. (British Columbia Paraplegic Association, n.d.: 1)

It is estimated that there are between 183,000 and 230,000 individuals with spinal cord injury in the US, with the incidence of SCI (not including those who die at the scene of the accident) being approximately 11,000 new cases annually (National Spinal Cord Injury Statistical Centre, 2001). The Department of Health in England reported a total of 16,983 hospital consultant episodes for SCI between 2002 and 2003 (WrongDiagnosis, n.d.). In South Africa, however, there are no official statistics on SCI. The 2001 Census report indicated that 5 percent of the population in South Africa were disabled; however, this included the various types of disabilities, viz. sight, hearing, communication, physical, intellectual and emotional disability. A total of 29.6 percent of the disabled population in South Africa presented with a physical disability (Statistics South Africa, 2005). According to the regional director of the QuadPara Association of South Africa, it is estimated that the incidence for SCI in South Africa from September 2003 to September 2004 is 650 (C. Hedgecock, personal communication, 9 May 2005).

Statistics at the Provincial Spinal Rehabilitation Centre (PSRC) in KwaZulu-Natal have shown that there are an increasing number of patients with SCI, mainly young male adults between 18 to 30 years. This is similar to national trends (Quadriplegic Association of South Africa, Pamphlet, n.d.: 6). A total of 111 SCI patients were admitted between 2003 to 2004. Forty-four percent of these patients were female (PSRC-KZN, Statistics, 2005). Internationally, fewer female than male SCI patients are also reported (Spinal Cord Injury Information Network, 2004; British Columbia Paraplegic Association, n.d.). These figures reveal that approximately 80 percent newly injured SCI patients are male (British Columbia Paraplegic Association, n.d.: 1). However, the Spinal Cord Injury Information Network (August, 2004) reported that there is a decreasing trend male spinal cord injured patients after the 1980s.

In the US, 50.4 percent of all spinal cord injuries resulted from motor vehicle accidents. The second leading cause of SCI were falls (23.8 percent), followed by acts of violence (primarily gunshot wounds), and recreational sporting activities such as diving (Spinal Cord Injury Facts, 2004: 2; National Spinal Cord Injury Association, n.d.: 1). A similar aetiological trend is evident in South Africa (QASA/Department of Health Database, 2005). However, acts of violence such as gunshot wounds are the second most common cause of SCIs after motor vehicle accidents. In addition, the motor vehicle accidents are mainly taxi-related (PSRC-KZN, Statistics 2002–2006).

Depression and SCI

Knowledge and the understanding of psychological aspects of spinal cord injury (SCI) are a neglected area in health. One of the most common forms of psychological distress in SCI patients is depressive disorders (Krause, Kemp & Coker, 2000). Patients with SCI experience many physical, functional and emotional losses (Boekamp, Overholser & Schubert, 1996; Nielsen, 2003). According to Boekamp et al. (1996) the consequences of SCI *inter alia* involve loss of motor function, loss of sensation, loss of control over bowel and bladder function, and impaired sexual functioning, all of which lead to changes in vocational roles, financial insecurity and disrupted interpersonal relationships. When disability causes loss of function, the individual is often faced with a series of gradual and insidious losses which cause a prolonged grief reaction (Jansen, 1985). Krupp (1976) quoted in Jansen (1985) states that this is the most difficult grieving process because of the continued and long-term loss of functioning and hope for recovery. Working with SCI patients is further complicated by the poor prognosis for recovery of motor function. Jansen (1985) stressed that continued support from loved ones is important, as the balancing of acceptance of lost functioning and potential with realistic hope for as full a life as possible, is very difficult. However, acceptance of the decreased potential and opportunity gives rise to increased possibilities for utilizing remaining capacities to the fullest extent (Jansen, 1985).

A large number of spinal cord injuries are traumatic in nature, i.e. motor vehicle accidents or acts of violence. In such instances, often family members or close friends are killed or injured as well, which results in an even greater sense of loss. There are many factors that may contribute to depression in patients after a spinal cord injury. Boekamp et al. (1996) have proposed a diathesis-stress model (Figure 1) to explain these factors.

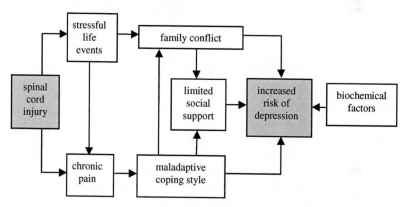

Figure 9.1. Diathesis-Stress Model Showing the Factors Influencing Risk of Depression Following a Spinal Cord Injury (Boekamp et al, 1996).

According to this model, biochemical factors associated with the injury, chronic pain and the frequency of stressful life events can increase the individual's risk of depression following a SCI. However, numerous psychological and social factors can intervene. Following the injury, the individual's coping styles may influence the vulnerability to stressful life events. In addition, the individual's adjustment may be strained by the limited availability of social support and/or the presence of family conflict (Boekamp et al, 1996).

Kennedy and Rogers (2000) found in a longitudinal analysis of anxiety and depression after SCI that the longer patients stayed in a hospital environment, the more depressed and anxious they became. According to Krause et al. (2000), individuals with low education, from minority backgrounds and older at the time of the SCI may be particularly vulnerable to depression.

Twenty percent of patients with longstanding physical illness may also suffer from significant depression, and the depressive symptoms can be difficult to distinguish from those of the physical illness (Hallstrom & McClure, 2005). According to Adler (2002) individuals who experience a sudden trauma that causes or necessitates amputations are likely to experience profound psychological shock, disbelief, and subsequently feelings of hopelessness, despondency, bitterness and anger.

In a study on suicidal ideation after life-threatening physical illnesses, for example stroke, traumatic brain injury, myocardial infarction and spinal cord injury, Kishi, Robinson and Kosier (2001) found that about 20 percent of patients developed suicidal ideation sometime within the two years following the illness. These authors also found that suicidal ideation during the acute medical treatment period was associated with the presence of a diagnosable depressive disorder.

Depression in Women

Independent of country or culture, there is a twofold greater prevalence of MDD in woman than in men (Kaplan & Sadock, 1998). There are many theories that explain women's susceptibility to depression, ranging from biological theories related to the role of hormones in women's moods to social theories that emphasise the effects of oppression in women and the consequences on their mental health, to psychological theories associated with the influence of women's personality traits (Nolen-Hoeksema, 1990). Kaplan and Sadock (1998) explain that hormonal differences, the effects of childbirth, differing psychosocial stressors for men and for women, and behavioural models of learned helplessness contribute to depression in woman. Nolen-Hoeksema argues that the absence of clear cultural differences in the rates of depression in men and women suggest that some factor universal to all women, such as a biological factor, predispose them to depression (1990: 36).

According to Hallstrom and McClure (2005), men often have their depression diagnosed as problems associated with alcohol or personality problems and they tend to project their suffering outwards. Women, on the other hand, are culturally allowed to express their suffering and tend to seek help more than men. The factors that make woman more vulnerable to depression include having three or more children under fifteen years of age at home, not working outside the home, the lack of a supportive relationship, with a husband and the loss of a mother through death or separation before the age of 11 (Hallstrom & McClure, 2005).

Women experience losses and tragedies throughout their lives, and a grief reaction can be triggered by death, separation and divorce, children leaving home, miscarriage and the agonizing pain of losing a child (Zisook, Chentsova-Dutton & Shuchter, 2000). Similarly, a grief reaction can also be triggered after an SCI from a loss of motor functioning. The stages of grief range from an initial period of shock, denial, numbness, and confusion to a period of acute grief and mourning where intense feelings of despair and anger are felt and social withdrawal occurs (Ibid.). This is similar to the stages of grief a person who has recently suffered an SCI undergoes. Very often a complicated grief reaction which takes place when the grief reaction is absent, delayed, intensified or prolonged also occurs with SCI individuals (Ibid.).

Socioeconomic factors also play a significant role. In South Africa, many women are single parents. Often cultural and economic factors force men to leave their homes and seek employment in the bigger cities: this has led to a breakdown in the family unit. This problem is further exacerbated by the effects of HIV and AIDS. The loss of a spouse, according Zisook, Chentsova-Dutton and Shuchter is a tragic and traumatic event that affects a woman's health, mood, social and spiritual life, deprives her of companionship and often depletes her financial resources and forces her to alter her established lifestyle (2000: 84). Many women are forced to raise their children by themselves and adopt the role of the homemaker. For such women an SCI is a double tragedy which results in loss of stability in the home environment.

Until recently, psychologists have shown very little interest in physical disability (Wilkinson, 1989). In South Africa very few psychologists have experience of working with patients with SCI. A review of the literature shows that there is a paucity of studies and information on the psychological issues among SCI patients in South Africa. This study therefore attempted to contribute to this dearth by determining the prevalence and gender differences of depression in a group of SCI patients at a rehabilitation unit.

Method

All patients admitted to a provincial spinal rehabilitation unit for a one (June 2002 and June 2003) were included in the study. A semi-structured interview and the Beck's Depression Inventory (BDI) were administered. A diagnosis of depression was made using the Diagnostic and Statistical

Manual of Mental Disorders, fourth edition, text revised (DSM IV-TR) criteria (APA, 2004). Data was captured on a MS Excel spreadsheet and statistical analysis was done using the statistical package SPSS version 15.

Subjects. The sample consisted of sixty-five patients. Fifty patients (76.92 percent) were paraplegic, while five (7.69 percent) were quadriplegic. Of the remaining patients, ten (15.38 percent) presented with hemiplegia, monoparesis or paraparesis. Forty-seven patients (72.31 percent) were male and eighteen (27.69 percent) were female (t=22.829, df 64, sig.000). The majority of patients (fifty-six) were Black African (86.20 percent); there were six Indians (9.20 percent) and three Whites (4.60 percent) in the sample group. See Table 1 for a breakdown according to gender. Occupations ranged from labourers, security guards and drivers to nurses and teachers. Many of the patients were drivers of cars, taxis, ambulances or forklifts. Women generally had lower levels of education: eleven (61 percent) had primary education and seven (38 percent) had secondary education, whereas among the male patients, fifteen (31 percent) had primary education and thirty-one (66 percent) had a secondary education. Women also had lower income levels.

Table 9.1. Gender and Ethnicity

	Female	Male	Total
Black	16 (88.90)	40 (85.10)	56 (86.15)
Indian	2 (11.10)	4 (8.50)	6 (9.23)
White		3 (6.4)	3 (4.61)
Total	18	47	65

Results

Based on DSM IV-TR criteria, a total of forty (61.5 percent) had a primary diagnoses of major depressive disorder (MDD), three (4.6 percent) an adjustment disorder (AD), three (4.6 percent) had mental retardation or borderline IQ, and for eighteen (27.7 percent) no diagnosis was made. Of those diagnosed with MDD, twenty-seven (67.5 percent) were male and thirteen (32.5 percent) were female. The BDI could only be administered to forty patients: thirty-two (80 percent) males and eight females (20 percent). The BDI identified thirty-five (87.5 percent) patients as depressed, twenty-seven (67.5 percent) males and eight (20 percent) females (see Table 2 for a further breakdown according to severity of depression). The mean BDI score for females was 23.63 (SD 12.212) and for males 19.69 (SD 10.316). While the means are not significantly different, the mean for the female group was higher. Of the eight females who were identified as depressed on the BDI, three (37.50 percent) were mildly depressed, three (37.50 percent) moderate and two (25.00 percent) severely depressed. The highest score on the BDI was a female.

Table 9.2. BDI Scores

Severity	Male n (%)	Female n (%)	Total n (%)
No or minimal depression	6 (18.75)	0	6 (15.00)
Mild Depression	11 (34.37)	3 (37.50)	14 (35.00)
Moderate Depression	9 (28.12)	3 ((37.50)	11 (27.50)
Severe depression	7 (21.87)	2 (25.00	9 (22.50)
Total	32	8	40

Discussion

More female SCI injured patients than male spinal cord injured patients presented with MDD. In the general population, twice as many women presented with depression as men; in general clinical settings it is much higher. At a psychological clinic in South Africa, the gender ratio for black Africans was four females to one male (Ngcobo & Pillay, 2008). However, little is known about depression in SCI patients in South Africa. In a study on depression after SCI, Krause et al. (2000) found that minority participants, especially women, are at a greater risk for depression, and that education and income largely accounted for the elevated risk for such individuals. A study of black African women attending a psychological clinic in South Africa for depression were also found to be single, unemployed, of low education and low income status. However, depression in the African community is often not a primary concern and its presentation is often neglected. The majority of patients live in poverty and struggle with complex economic issues as a result of homelessness, domestic violence, etc. Most of their energy is spent meeting basic needs such as food, housing, and employment for themselves and their families, which take priority over depression (Ngcobo & Pillay, 2008). However, given the roles and responsibilities of women in the community, SCI presents a serious disruption and it is unimaginable the impact that these disruptions has on their mental health not only of the women but on their family and communities as well.

Although more females presented with MDD than males, five out of the seven patients who were suicidal were male. While female SCI patients expressed their depression, male SCI patients are less expressive in revealing symptoms of depression and may act out their despair and hopelessness by wanting to end their lives.

Some patients are able to cope and adjust to their condition despite their severe injuries, whilst others struggle. This may be explained by a combination of factors such as an individual's pre-morbid personality, "locus of control", family and friends support or the lack thereof, socio-economic status, the attitudes and personalities of the health personnel (and other patients) with whom they come into contact at the time of their hospitalization and rehabilitation, and their emotional and spiritual intelligence.

Conclusion

The results of this study suggest that women with SCIs experience many losses after the injury and are at a great risk of suffering from depression. For many rural South African women, the greatest sense of loss is the traditional role of being the mother and the anchor in her family. Her responsibilities of caring for her children, husband and elders is reversed: she now is in need of care. In a paper on psychotherapy for depression, Karasu (1990) explains that in the interpersonal approach the use of losses as opportunities for new possibilities and growth is important. Such an approach, as part of an eclectic orientation, is crucial when dealing with SCI patients, especially women. The loss should be construed as an avenue for women suffering SCIs to discover and realize new potentials, abilities, strengths and resources within themselves for further empowerment.

Bibliography

Adler, C. "Spinal Cord Injury." In L. W. Pedretti and M. B. Early, eds., *Occupational Therapy: Practise Skills for Physical Dysfunction*. New York, NY: Mosby, 2002.

American Psychiatric Association. *Diagnostic and Statistical Manual of Mental Disorders (DSM-IV)*. Fourth Edition. Washington, D.C.: APA, 1994.

Boekamp, J. R., J. C. Overholser and D. S. P. Schubert. "Depression Following a Spinal Cord Injury." *International Journal of Psychiatry in Medicine*, 26 no. 3 (1996): 329–349.

British Columbia Paraplegic Association. (n.d.). Retrieved 28 April 2005 from http://www.island.net/~bcpa/sci.html

Hallstrom, C., and N. McClure. *Depression. Your Questions Answered.* Edinburgh, Scotland: Elsevier, 2005.

Jansen, M. A. "Psychotherapy and Grieving: A Clinical Approach." In E. M. Stern, ed., *Psychotherapy and the Grieving Patient.* New York, NY: Haworth Press, 1985.

Kaplan, H., and B. Sadock. *Kaplan and Sadock's Synopsis of Psychiatry: Behavioural Sciences, Clinical Psychiatry.* Eighth Edition. London, England: Lippincott, Williams and Wilkins, 1998.

Karasu, T. B. "Psychotherapy for Depression." *American Journal of Psychiatry*, 147 (1990): 141.

Karause, J. S., B. Kemp and J. Coker. "Depression after Spinal Cord Injury: Relation to Gender, Ethnicity, Aging, and Socioeconomic Indicators." *Archives of Physical Medicine and Rehabilitation*, 81 (2000): 1099–1109.

Kennedy, P., and Ben A. Rogers. "Anxiety and Depression after Spinal Cord Injury: A Longitudinal Analysis. *Archives of Physical Medicine and Rehabilitation*, 81 (2000): 932–937.

Kishi, Y., R. G. Robinson and J. T. Kosier. "Suicidal Ideation among Patients During the Rehabilitation Period after Life-Threatening Physical Illness." *The Journal of Mental and Physical Disease.* 189 no. 9 (2001): 623–628.

Lustig, D. C. "The Adjustment Process for Individuals with Spinal Cord Injury: The Effect of Perceived Premorbid Sense of Coherence." *Rehabilitation Counseling Bulletin*, 48 no. 3 (2005): 146–156.

National Spinal Cord Injury Association Resource Centre. "Fact Sheet no. 2: Spinal Cord Injury Statistics." (n.d.). Retrieved 27 May 2005 from http://www.makoa.org/nscia/fact02.html

National Spinal Cord Injury Statistical Centre. "Facts and Figures at a Glance—May 2001." (2001) Retrieved 15 November 2003 from http://www.spinal cord.uab.edu/show.asp?durki=21446

Ngcobo, M., and B. J. Pillay. "Depression in African Women Presenting for Psychological Services at a General Hospital." *African Journal of Psychiatry* (May, 2008): 133–137.

Nielsen, M. S. Post-Traumatic Stress Disorder and Emotional Distress in Persons with Spinal Cord Lesion. *Spinal Cord*, 41 (2003): 296–302.

Nolen-Hoeksema, S. *Sex Differences in Depression.* Palo Alto, CA: Stanford University Press, 1990.

Quadriplegic Association of South Africa. "QASA Believes that Life Needn't Stop When You're Paralyzed." P6. (n.d).

Spinal Cord Injury Facts. "Spinal Cord Injury Statistics." August, 2004. Retrieved 27 May 2005 from http://www.fscip.org/facts.htm

Spinal Cord Injury Information Network. "Facts and Figures at a Glance." (August, 2004). Retrieved 30 April 2005, from http://.spinalcord.uab. edu/show.asp?durki=21446

Spinal Cord Injury Resources. (n.d.) Retrieved 28 April 2005 from http:// www.spinal-cord-linjuy-resources.com/spinal-types.html

Statistics South Africa. "Census 2001." *Prevalence of Disability in South Africa.* Report no. 03-02-44. Pretoria, South Africa: Statistics South Africa, 2005. Retrieved 2 May 2005 from http://www.statssa.gov.za

Wilkinson, S. M. "Psychological Aspects of Physical Disability." in A. K. Broome, ed., *Health Psychology: Processes and Applications.* New York, NY: Chapman and Hall, 1989.

Wrong Diagnosis. "Introduction: Spinal Cord Disorders." n.d. Retrieved 28 April 2005 from http://www.wrongdiagnosis.com/s/spinal_cord_ disorders/intro.htm

Zisook, S., Y. Chentsova-Dutton and S. R. Shuchter. "Grief and Bereavement in Woman." In M. Steiner, K. A. Yonkers, and E. Eriksson, eds., *Mood Disorders in Woman.* London, England: Martin Dunitz Ltd., 2000.

"PORPHYRIA MAKES ME DEPRESSED"

KAREN NOONAN AND ISABELLE ELLIS

Introduction

Depression is very common; it is the fourth leading cause of disease burden in Australia, accounting for 4 percent of the total burden of disease (Mathers, Vos & Stevenson 1999: 65). Porphyria, on the other hand, is a relatively rare metabolic disorder, the incidence being one in 100,000 in the adult population and one in 250 in the mental health population (Tishler et al. 1985). Porphyria often presents as depression. In this chapter we will present three case stories: these cases will illustrate the importance of appropriate testing to identify if depression or other psychiatric conditions are in fact symptoms of porphyria. Psychiatric symptoms of porphyria are often made worse by the common treatments used mistakenly for acute depression or psychosis. Porphyria is not curable, but the symptoms can be successfully managed.

Karen's Story

From the age of thirty-two Karen suffered from repeated non-specific episodes of abdominal pain, nausea and vomiting. Just prior to her diagnosis when she was thirty-four, she was experiencing visual disturbances. She would see three little silhouette creatures: a mouse, a spider and a snake. Although at that time she could discern that these images were not real, it was at times frustrating because she knew something was going on. She was frightened and went repeatedly to the doctor to be told there was nothing wrong, "its stress". During that time Karen became depressed and withdrawn. Although never diagnosed as being clinically depressed, there were times where she felt really low and withdrawn. Karen continued to have symptoms: chronic non-specific abdominal pain, nausea, vomiting, and at times she craved carbohydrates (things like fresh bread, or a bowl of plain boiled pasta).

In 2001 Karen was finally diagnosed with Hereditary Coproporphyria. Neither of her parents had any idea that they had porphyria in their family.

Both of Karen's parents lived in different states at the time and were both told by their GPs that porphyria is so rare that their daughter must be misdiagnosed. Their GPs did not initially test either of Karen's parents.

During her search for a diagnosis, Karen was subjected to a barrage of tests, including a laparoscopy that found nothing. Doctors had prescribed metaclopramide and other drugs to treat her continued nausea and vomiting, and oxycodone and tramil to treat her abdominal pain. It wasn't until she went to see a gastroenterologist that the symptoms were all put together and she was finally tested for porphyria. After three days the tests came back positive, and then the search for information began in earnest. The doctor told her that the disease was incredibly rare; however, there was one famous sufferer, King George III of England. The doctor ceased the drug regimen that Karen had been prescribed and commenced "safe medications" namely panadeine forte, naprosyn for pain management and proclorperazine for nausea and vomiting.

What is Known of King George III's Story

King George III, one of the longest-reigning kings of England suffered from well-documented psychoses. These psychotic episodes have been described as "periods of insanity". The best-documented episode was from November 1788 to February 1789, which precipitated the constitutional review known as the Regency Crisis. From the detailed recorded history, Macalpine and Hunter hypothesised that King George had porphyria (Cox, Jack, Lofthouse, Watling, Haines & Warren, 2005). His history shows that when he was unwell, in addition to psychoses, he also experienced abdominal pain, polyneuropathies, tachycardia, changes in bowel function and dark urine. These symptoms subsided during times of wellness. A follow-up study by Macalpine and Hunter of King George III's forebears, descendants and collateral relatives shows that he most probably suffered variegate porphyria, which was diagnosed in 1969 in his direct descendent Prince William of Gloucester. King George's acute episodes were of unusually long duration. A recent study of King George's hair show that he may have been made worse by the commonly used treatment administered by the King's physicians of emetic tartar, two grains, every six hours (Ibid.).

An Oscar-award-winning movie called "The Madness of King George" directed by Nicholas Hytner was released in 1995, and as a result porphyria has become known as "the mad disease". Consequently many people believe porphyria to be a psychotic condition, when in fact many sufferers are asymptomatic and still others have no psychiatric symptoms.

As a result of the link with possible psychiatric symptoms, porphyria now has a negative stigma attached. A recent episode of a popular crime scene investigation series gave the villain, a psychopath, a diagnosis of porphyria.

Jane's Story

The following case story was published in the *Journal of Psychiatric Practice* in 2002. Jane was a thirty-one-year old mother of three. She had a long history of mood lability and had received intermittent psychiatric treatment for depression and suicide ideation. Jane became a voluntary admission to the locked psychiatric unit when her partner became increasingly concerned for her safety and that of their children. Jane's symptoms on admission included abdominal pain, anorexia, depressive symptoms, suicide ideation, and homicidal thoughts towards her children. She had been recently commenced on valproic acid, clonazepam, trazodone and zolpiderm by her GP for her depression and abdominal symptoms.

Jane had a known history of porphyria in her family: however, she was tested on admission for porphyria and the results at that time were negative. Despite the results, Jane's drug regimen was changed to promethazine and meperide for abdominal pain. She was commenced on 5 percent Dextrose by intravenous infusion and her other medications were discontinued, as any of these medications could have precipitated or exacerbated an attack of Acute Intermittent Porphyria. Jane's physical symptoms rapidly subsided and after a week she had no further psychiatric symptoms and was discharged on no medications (Croarkin, 2002).

What is Porphyria?

Porphyria is a metabolic condition that affects the blood. Everyone produces porphyrins in their body and most people naturally excrete them. However, a porphyria sufferer is unable to excrete these porphyrins so they build up in the body, causing the person to become toxic and unwell.

Porphyrins are produced in the biosynthetic pathway. The biosynthetic pathway is responsible for the production and processing of porphyrins. Porphyrins are needed to help make haem, a component of blood. To produce haem there are eight distinct stages or gates: a person with porphyria will have a defect at one of these stages or gates. The type of porphyria will be dependent on where in the stages or gates the defect occurs. Karen was diagnosed with hereditary coproporphyria, so she has a defect with the "coproporphyrinogen III" gate.

There are eight main types of porphyria: Acute Intermittent Porphyria (AIP), Congenital Porphyria Cutanea Tarda (PCT), Hereditary Copoporphyria (HCP), Variegate Porphyria (VP), Protoporphyria and Erythropoietic Protoporphyria (EPP), ALA dehratase-deficiency Porphyria (ALA) and Erythropoietic Porphyria (EEP or CEP). Acute Intermittent Porphyria (AIP) is considered to be the most common form of porphyria. It is an hereditary condition resulting from an autosomal dominant gene. It is affected by the enzyme PBG deaminase. A person who has AIP can have acute attacks and psychosis; generally there is no cutaneous involvement. AIP is considered to be the most severe of all types of porphyria, and generally literature will tell you that symptoms do not occur before puberty; however there has been a documented diagnosis on a young child—a two-year-old was diagnosed in Victoria (Andersson, Innala & Backstrom, 2003).

There are two types of Porphyria Cutanea Tarda (PCT), type 1 or acquired PCT, which accounts for 80 percent of those diagnosed with PCT, and type II or inherited PCT, which accounts for 20 percent of cases. PCT type II results from an autosomal dominant gene defect, which affects the uroporphyrinogen oxidase enzyme. PCT is known to cause underlying liver cell damage with iron overload (Koszo, Morvay, Dobozy & Simon, 1992). PCT is the only type of porphyria that can be both acquired and inherited: it is the most common type of acquired porphyria (Hussain, Hepburn, Jones, O'Rolrke & Hayes, 1996). There is a strong association between PCT type I and alcohol dependency, Hepatitis C and Human Immunodeficiency Virus (HIV) infection. Literature tells us that there are a significant number of people with PCT type I who have developed Hep C and/or HIV, and people with these diseases have developed PCT type I (Ibid.). PCT has also been called the "Gulf War Syndrome". American soldiers on return from the first Gulf War displayed symptoms of porphyria: on further investigation they were found to be positive for PCT type I (Unwin, Blatchley, Coker, Ferry, Hotopf, Hull et al., 1999). Here in Australia there is no documentation to verify if our defence force personnel are routinely tested on return from active duty. However, the Vietnam Veterans' Association has listed PCT as one of the compensable conditions resulting from exposure to Agent Orange in the Vietnam War.

Hereditary Coproporhyria (HCP) is considered the least common types of porphyria, and very little is known about it. It is affected by the coproporphyriogen oxidase enzyme and is an autosomal dominant trait, which means that one parent has to carry the defective gene and this has a 50 percent chance of being passed on to offspring, equally between male and female. Hereditary coproporphyria has acute symptoms, psychotic and cutaneous symptoms (Fraser & Longden, 2003).

Variegate Porphyria (VP) is the result of an autosomal dominant gene defect. The protoporphrinogen oxidase enzyme metabolism is affected. This type of porphyria supposedly does not have psychotic symptoms, but this has been increasingly debated in the literature. This is the kind of porphyria that King George III is now thought to have had. Photosensitive skin lesions are prevalent in 60 percent of VP sufferers, particularly on exposed skin; 20 percent have acute neurovisceral symptoms and the other 20 percent have a combination of cutaneous and acute symptoms. VP is very common in South Africa at an incident rate of one in 200 to 250 per population owing to a founder effect amongst Afrikaans (Hift, Meissner, Corrigall, Ziman, Petersen, Meissner et al., 1997).

Testing for Porphyria

Currently the testing for the initial diagnosis for all types of porphyria is a urine sample, blood test and a faecal specimen. Depending on the enzyme found in relevant samples, a diagnosis of type can be made. All these samples need to be protected from the light, as light denatures the porphyrins, resulting in a false negative result. Once a diagnosis has been made, a urine sample is used to determine if an acute attack is occurring. It is important that testing for porphyria be conducted at specialist laboratories: these can be found in every Australian State except for the Northern Territory.

It is well-documented that porphyria is one of the most under-diagnosed medical conditions. Kondo et al. (2004), from Japan conducted a study of all 827 known porphyria cases diagnosed by characteristic clinical or laboratory findings between 1920 and 2002 and found 71 percent of acute hepatic porphyria cases had been initially misdiagnosed and that a high percentage had a negative result on initial testing. On average it takes six years from initial symptoms to a definitive diagnosis.

Trigger Factors

As you can see from the stories of Karen, Jane and King George III, the drugs commonly used to treat symptoms were in fact triggering an acute episode of porphyria, or making them worse. There are many triggers that can cause an attack. Illicit drugs, alcohol, foods such as tomatoes, red grapes, red wine and port are particularly unsafe for a porphyria sufferer. Soy products have been found to be unsafe. Many heavy metals such as lead, mercury and arsenic are known triggers. Stress, illness and infections can also trigger an attack.

There are many medications that are considered to be unsafe, and generally a person who has been diagnosed with porphyria will carry a list with them that states the medications that they should not have. It is very important that unsafe medications are not given, even if these previously had no negative effect. Unsafe medications have been known to cause bulbar paralysis, which is paralysis of the respiratory tract (Croarkin, 2002). Generally the reason that these medications are unsafe is because they work on an enzyme known as cytochrome P450. This enzyme stimulates the biosynthetic pathway, thus causing more porphyrins to be produced and therefore causing an attack. Common unsafe medications include diazepam, zoloft, chlorpromazine, clonazepam, midazolam, promethazine, metoclopramide and avanza.

The hormones oestrogen and progesterone have been shown to increase the porphyrin precursors by inducing the first enzyme in the biosynthesis of haem in women diagnosed with AIP. It is also documented that women often experience their first porphyria attack during pregnancy. Porphyria is associated with high rates of miscarriage (Andersson, Innala & Backstrom, 2003).

Symptoms

Symptoms of porphyria are very broad and each attack can be different from the last. Porphyria can affect all systems within the body. Porphyria usually present in three different ways: mental state changes, neurovisceral symptoms, cutaneous symptoms, or a combination of all three. Mental state changes are noted in 24 to 80 percent of cases of porphyria and psychotic symptoms and confusion are observed in 40 percent of these (Croarkin, 2002). Acute episodes can present with similar symptoms as depression, schizophrenia, anxiety and other mental disturbances. It is well-documented that porphyria has been misdiagnosed as schizophrenia and the diagnosis later changed to porphyria, as in Jane's case. Most, if not all people with porphyria will experience some form of depression at sometime during their illness. There are so many factors that contribute to this: being diagnosed with a chronic condition that appears to have very little known about it and no clear treatment protocols is just one of the factors that contribute to a sense of hopeless. Here in Australia, we are not aware of any clinical expert in treating porphyria and this makes it very hard for all concerned.

Millward, Kelly, King and Peters (2005) found that depression and anxiety were more common in porphyria patients than general population, anxiety being present as an underlying state rather than a transitory psychological problem secondary to acute porphyria. They found porphyria patients have an impaired quality of life and that those with AIP had an even lower quality of life than other porphyria sufferers. There were psychosocial implications, loss of employment and limitation of family size.

A porphyria patient can display neurovisceral symptoms such as abdominal pain, nausea, vomiting, paralysis and muscle weakness. Abdominal pain is considered the most common symptom, experienced by 90 to 95 percent of patients with porphyria. The pain is non-specific and so can be very difficult to diagnose, particularly if there are no suspicions of porphyria. It has been well documented that patients are put through unnecessary procedures such as laparoscopy and abdominal surgery. Cutaneous symptoms, such as skin blistering on exposure to the sun, are common presenting symptoms. Other common symptoms include tachycardia (a fast heart rate) and dark-coloured urine. These symptoms usually only occur when the person is having an attack and settle down in between. A person with porphyria can have one of these presentations or a combination of any of these. These symptoms tend to change and are not consistent with each attack.

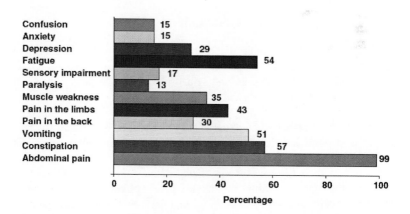

Figure 10.1. Frequency of Symptoms During the Acute Attack Reported by Ninety-One Women with Manifest AIP (Andersson, Innala & Backstrom, 2003: 178).

We believe that porphyria may be the underlying cause of many chronic conditions. As has been previously stated, it is well-documented that depression is part of porphyria and women are more likely to become symptomatic than men because of oestrogen production. A question to consider is whether women with postnatal depression are suffering from undiagnosed porphyria.

Treatment

Currently there is no known cure for porphyria, and treatment is controversial. Firstly, the diagnosis needs to be confirmed; when confirmation has been made, then it is usually a urine test or blood for EEP that will determine whether a patient is having an attack. Guidelines recommend intravenous glucose during an acute attack, as glucose binds to the porphyrins. Porphyria sufferers require a high carbohydrate diet of at least 300 grams per day, increased to at least 600 gms per day when unwell. If this doesn't work, then intravenous hemin or hemin arginate are commenced. This is a synthetic form of heam that is produced in the biosynthetic pathway. This has many sideeffects and can cause phlebitis and inflammation of the veins (Blackburn & Jensen, 1994). It is important to stop all known triggers, whether or not a reaction has previously occurred.

Conclusion

Porphyria is a metabolic disorder caused by an over-production of porphyrins. It can mimic some forms of psychosis and is often misdiagnosed as schizophrenia and schizo-effective disorders. There is a high incident of misdiagnosis and non diagnosis. Porphyria suffers need to be aware of and keep away from triggers. A high carbohydrate diet, increasing even further when experiencing symptoms, is required. Not all people with porphyria develop symptoms; they can remain asymptomatic for life. On the other hand, others develop symptoms and may have only one attack in their life time or may have many. A correct diagnosis will decrease the burden within the health care system, especially when patients are being treated incorrectly for an illness that they do not have.

Recommendations

1. There is a need to raise awareness of porphyria, educate patients, family, health workers and the community.

2. When porphyria is suspected, it needs to be tested and retested for.

3. There is a need for further research into the experience of living with porphyria.

Bibliography

Andersson, C., E. Innala and T. Backstrom. "Acute Intermittent Porphyria in Women: Clinical Expression, Use and Experience of Exogenous Sex Hormones. A Population-Based Study in Northern Sweden." *Journal of Internal Medicine*, no. 254 (2003): 176–83.

Blackburn, G., and G. Jensen. "Nutrition Management of Acute Intermittent Porphyria." *Nutrition*, 10 no. 6 (1994): 551–6.

Cox, T., N. Jack, S. Lofthouse, J. Watling, J. Haines and M. Warren. "King George III and Porphyria: An Elemental Hypothesis and Investigation." *The Lancet*, 366 no. 9482 (2005): 332–5.

Croarkin, P. "From King George to Neuroglobin: The Psychiatric Aspects of Acute Intermittent Porphyria." *Journal of Psychiatric Practice*, 8 no. 6 (2002): 398–405.

Fraser, J., and P. Longden. "The Atkins Diet as a Possible Trigger for an Acute ICU Admission: A Case Report." *Critical Care and Resuscitation*, no. 5 (2003): 193–7.

Hift, R., P. Meissner, A. Corrigall, M. Ziman, L. Petersen, D. Meissner, B. Davidson, J. Sutherland, H. Dailey and R. Kirsch. "Variegate Porphyria in South Africa, 1688–1996—New Developments in an Old Disease." *South African Medical Journal*, 87 no. 6 (1997): 722–31.

Hussain, I., N. Hepburn, A. Jones, K. O'Rolrke and P. C. Hayes. "The Association of Hepatitis C Viral Infection with Pyphoria Cutanea Tarda in the Lothian Region of Scotland." *Clinical and Experimental Dermatology*, 21 no. 4 (1996): 283–5.

Kondo, M., Y. Yano, M. Shirataka, G. Uurata and S. Sassa. "Porphyrias in Japan: Compilation of All Cases Reported through 2002." *International Journal of Hematology*, 79 no. 5 (2004): 448–56.

Koszo, F., M. Morvay, A. Dobozy and N. Simon. "Erythrocyte Uroporphyrinogen Decarboxylase Activity in 80 Unrelated Patients with Porphuyria Cutanea Tarda." *British Journal of Dermatology*, 126 no. 5 (1992): 446–9.

Mathers, C., T. Vos and C. Stevenson. *The Burden of Disease and Injury in Australia*. cat. no. PHE 17, AIHW. Canberra, Australia: 1999.

Millward, L., P. Kelly, A. King and T. Peters. "Anxiety and Depression in Acute Porphyrias." *Journal of Inherited Metabolic Disease*, 28 no. 6 (2005): 1099–107.

Tishler, P. V., B. Woodward, J. O'Connor, D. A. Holbrook, L. J. Seidman, M. Hallett and D. J. Knighton. "High Prevalence of Intermittent Acute Porphyria in a Psychiatric Patient Population." *American Journal of Psychiatry*, no. 142 (1985): 1430–6.

Unwin, C., N. Blatchley, W. Coker, S. Ferry, M. Hotopf, L. Hull, K. Ishmail, I. Palmer, A. David and S. Wessely. "Health of UK Servicemen who Served in Persian Gulf War." *Lancet*, 353 no. 9148 (1999): 169–78.

THE MISSING LINK:
WOMEN, DEPRESSION
AND MIDLIFE TRANSITION

ROBYN VICKERS-WILLIS

This essay proposes that in Western culture there is much misunderstanding and misinformation about the role depression can play in a woman's midlife period—that is from the ages of thirty-five to fifty years—as she navigates the significant adult developmental stage of midlife transition.

Drawing on Jungian psychology and my own research on midlife development, this essay explains why the midlife period is a time of significant psychological and spiritual development for a woman, a time when it is vital for her to embrace her feelings rather than sedate or run away from them, if she is to create a personally meaningful second half of life. Drawing on published research on women and depression, this essay also considers the impact of the omission of context from much of the current thinking on depression and the role "the language of depression" plays in midlife women's lives "to articulate an embodied emotional crisis of identity and meaning in their lives" (Fullagar, 2008: 40).

It all started in my mid-thirties. I was angry, depressed and lethargic with swinging energy levels, increasing muscle tension and gynaecological problems. I was bewildered. What was happening to me? A gynaecologist suggested I take Hormone Replacement Therapy; however, with my mother's history of breast cancer in her early forties I knew this was not wise. There were continual visits to the doctor, and then referral to a psychiatrist who subscribed anti-depressants which numbed all my feelings. Then I was referred to a psychologist in whom I had no confidence, but I felt too desperate to stop going.

On the surface all looked fine. I was married to a hard-working man, had three healthy children, was financially secure with a lovely home and a career as a psychologist. What could possibly be wrong with me? Was I going crazy? Finally it all came to a head on my fortieth birthday, when I experienced what is commonly referred to as a midlife crisis.

I remember walking down the passage and in to the dining room where the well-wishers were. I was numb with despair, and dumb with terror. Did they notice? I attempted a smile. I moved through the room. I was a skin with nothing inside. I had to keep going through the motions. I couldn't let anybody know. Could they see my emptiness? Could they feel my emptiness? Could I keep it up? How long to go?

By luck, the next day I was referred to a health professional who listened to me, and as he did he helped me to start accepting my feelings of anger, sadness and lethargy and my desire for change. I started navigating what I now regard as the most significant psychological journey in a woman's life—midlife transition. Soon my health problems disappeared.

Since that time many years ago and now after years of research and writing on midlife development it has become clear to me that in our Western culture there is a missing link in the way a midlife woman's wellbeing is portrayed. This missing link means there is much misunderstanding and misinformation about the role of depression for women at midlife—that is from the ages of thirty-five to fifty years—as they navigate the significant adult developmental stage of midlife transition.

There is such a focus on a woman's bodily changes at midlife, and in particular on her hormonal changes, that her important psychological development at this time of life has been completely overlooked. An example of how strong is this mindset is that when my first book, *Navigating Midlife: Women Becoming Themselves* was first sent out to the media, my publisher had to write on a red sheet of paper in large black letters "this is not a book about menopause".

Midlife Transition

Carl Jung (1875–1961), the renowned Swiss psychologist, said that the life cycle is archetypal, meaning that all human beings are born with an inbuilt blue-print for development where the life cycle is made up of a series of mini-deaths and births at significant developmental life transitions. Jung proposed that these patterns of becoming are built into the psyche from the moment of conception leading through nine months in the womb to the first birth. Jung then said there was the death of childhood and a second birth at puberty followed by adolescent transition leading in to adulthood with a third birth occurring at midlife, followed by midlife transition leading in to the second half of life (Jung, 1985: 109–131).

Through observations of both himself and his patients, Jung came to the conclusion that individuation was the primary task of the second half of life defining individuation as:

> the process by which individual beings are formed and differentiated; in particular it is the development of the psychological *individual* (q.v.) as a being distinct from the general, collective psychology. Individuation, therefore, is a process of *differentiation* (q.v.), having for its goal the development of the personality. (Jung, 1971: 448)

Jung said that for normal psychological development, in the first half of life we create a lifestyle and an understanding of who we are based on what parents, other significant adults, our peers, partners and society in general expect of us. This socialization enables us to feel secure as we learn to "fit in" to the environment we are born in to. As we experience this conditioning we come to understand that parts of us are not acceptable, and these parts we repress deep in our unconscious. Jung went on to say that for normal psychological development in the second half of life, we need to create a life based on who we truly are, and to do this we need to complete two main developmental tasks for midlife transition. First, we need to find ways to connect with our inner world to reclaim those parts of ourselves repressed when young and other parts of our selves we have never known. And second, we need to create a lifestyle based on this increased understanding of who we truly are.

Jung was the first psychologist to acknowledge the significance of ongoing psychological development throughout the lifespan for healthy development of the personality (Stein, 1998: 172). Contrary to Sigmund Freud, who believed that early childhood experience strongly determined adult personality (McAdams, 1996), a significant number of social scientists have shown through their writing an alignment with Jung's understandings about adult development, and although they naturally do not agree on every point, Dan McAdams (Ibid., 2006), Else Frenkel (1936), David Gutmann (1987), Elliot Jaques (1965), Daniel Levinson (1978), Erik Erikson (1982) and Robert Kegan (1982) have all written about how people can experience important shifts in their life perspective as they evolve towards greater psychological maturity in their middle years.

From the 1980s American writer and researcher Gail Sheehy published several bestselling books on adult development (Sheehy, 1981, 1988). In contrast to much of the research and theories on adult development developed up until this stage, Sheehy focused on a broad cross-section of society, including women and non-professional men. This was an important shift, as so often in previous writing generalisations had been made about adult development based on research only carried out on white professional men (Gilligan, 1993: 5–23).

Given that men and women experience different socialization in the first half of life, an important new understanding that came with Sheehy's research was that what men and women seek for themselves in the second half of life may be very different, for as I found in my own research, what has been neglected in the first half of life seeks expression in the second half of life (Vickers-Willis, 2004: 17). Sheehy notes principal findings from longitudinal studies at the University of California, Berkeley:

> Both men and women who emerge psychologically healthiest at fifty are those who, as their goals and expectations change with age shape a "new self," that calls on qualities that were dormant earlier. This "new self" then fits in to a new life structure appropriate to the second half of adulthood. (Sheehy, 1995: 154)

Jung perceived midlife transition, in its deepest sense, as both a spiritual and a psychological journey where one goes on a quest to find one's soul, where "finding one's soul" (or Self in Jungian terms) involves confronting the unconscious, and integrating its elements into consciousness (Jung, 1985).

Jung conceptualised the stages of midlife transition as first the breakdown of the persona or the identity developed in the first half of life; second, the release of the shadow, meaning the release of those aspects of oneself which have been repressed, denied and rejected; third, integration of these shadow aspects; and fourth, facing and integrating the contra-sexual other—the animus, or inner "masculine" aspect of a woman and the anima, or inner "feminine" aspect of a man. All of these lead to a fuller and deeper understanding about oneself, creating the foundation for a personally meaningful second half of life based on one's own values (Stein, 1983: 26).

This time of psychological and spiritual awakening can for some lead to dramatic, sudden shifts in the psyche, especially in the initial stages of midlife transition, leading to what is popularly referred to as a midlife-crisis, an experience that is trivialized, under-researched and little understood in Western culture.

Although the word *crisis*, derived from the Greek word *krino* and meaning "to decide" (Alexander, 1978: 8), may be an accurate word to describe this turning point experienced by many at the initial stages of midlife transition, because the word "crisis" is not well understood in Western culture and the term "midlife crisis" is a target for ridicule, the association of crisis with midlife can create a mindset that this midlife experience is something to fear, to avoid, to repress. And given the focus on a woman's bodily changes at midlife, and in particular on her hormonal changes, her experience of "difficult feelings" at midlife is easily dismissed by responses such as "it's just her hormones", while her important psychological development at this time of life is easily overlooked. These stereotypical ways of viewing midlife change can cause even further anxiety to women at midlife as they feel from within a need to make significant changes in how they perceive themselves and how they choose to live their life.

Stein talks about a "crack" opening in one's identity at midlife, a crack that appears between the person one has perceived oneself to be in one's own eyes and in the eyes of others, and the person one now starts to sense one truly is (1983: 33). He goes on to say that as terrifying as the experience of this sudden crack in the identity is, it is often the best way forward, for otherwise natural defences pull the individual back into his or her first half of life identity, even though it will now appear a little false. This crack is the shift from a persona-orientation to a Self-orientation, and according to Stein, is

> critical for the individuation process as a whole, because it is the change by which a person sheds layers of familial and cultural influence and attains to some degree of uniqueness in (her) appropriation of internal and external facts and influences. (Ibid., 27)

In his cross-cultural studies on mythology, Joseph Campbell found in virtually all cultures stories about a quest for meaning and transformation during adulthood (1973: 245). There is also a wealth of literary and biographical material in Western writing on this quest for meaning and transformation for midlife transition—tales of epic journeys such as Homer's *Odyssey* and Dante's *The Divine Comedy* are rich metaphors for this "dark night of the soul" journey, while contemporary portrayals are found in the novels, biographies, plays, films and poetry of the modern era.

Prose is often an expression and reflection of the writer's own inner struggle as he or she enters into or is in the midst of this midlife experience. For example, Dante was aged thirty-five years in the year 1300 when he wrote in *The Divine Comedy*: "Midway this way of life we're bound upon / I woke to find myself in a dark wood / Where the right road was wholly lost and gone...." (1961: lines 1–3). Mary Oliver was forty-two years old when she wrote in *The Journey*: "One day you finally knew / what you had to do, and began, / though the voices around you / kept shouting / their bad advice...." (1986: lines 1–5). Therefore Jung did not create this understanding of the midlife crisis or midlife transition;

however, he was the first person to give this midlife experience psychological meaning when he wrote in the 1930s:

> Statistical tables show a rise in the frequency of cases of mental depression in men about forty. In women the neurotic difficulties generally begin somewhat earlier. We see that in this phase of life—between thirty-five and forty—a significant change in the human psyche is in preparation. At first it is not a conscious and striking change; it is rather a matter of indirect signs of a change which seems to take its rise from the unconscious. (1985: 120)

When a woman visits her GP presenting with some of these "indirect signs", the GP will draw on a diagnostic manual such as the *Diagnostic and Statistical Manual of Mental Disorders* (DSM-IV) (1992). It states that one has depression if over a two-week period one experiences five or more of the following symptoms, including at least one of the first two: a continuing and recurrent depressed mood; a markedly diminished interest or pleasure in most daily activities; change in eating habits; change in sleeping habits; nervous agitation or retardation; recurrent fatigue or loss of energy; feelings of worthlessness or inappropriate feelings of guilt; diminished inability to think, concentrate or make decisions; and recurrent thoughts of dying.

> In addition, the symptoms must cause clinically significant distress or impairment in significant areas of functioning ....and they must not be symptoms that are better explained by bereavement. (Polden, 2002: 226)

The World Health Organisation (WHO) projects that depression will be the second greatest global health problem by 2020 and is currently one of the major issues affecting women (Fullagar, 2008: 36). In considering this statement it is important to acknowledge the impact of the medicalisation of depression early in the twentieth century as it became part of the psychiatric classification system. A recently published Australian paper to "explore the diverse range of descriptive and etiological theories that have been proposed to explain why more women than men are depressed" (Boughton & Street, 2007: 187) concludes that the medicalisation of depression has led to an over-focus on the intra-psychic functioning of the depressed person at the expense of considering the social context in which depression occurs. They give as an example how behaviours such as "crying" and "loss of interest in sex" are used as measures of depression, with the inevitable result that women are over-identified as depressed. It is also important to note that although significantly more women than men are diagnosed with depression in their middle years, alcoholism rates for men are the mirror opposite:

> When the greater tendency of men to anaesthetize their moods by drinking or submerge themselves obsessively in work is taken into account, along with men's much greater reluctance to come forward to get help, the gender gap narrows dramatically. (Polden, 2002: 222)

Qualitative research by Kleiber, Hutchinson and Williams (2002) highlights the role emotions play in the process of transformation and the importance of women experiencing depression to explore alternative stories about self apart from the illness narrative. Different theories of depression do exist; however, the prominent pathway for recovery presented to women is pharmacological with a focus on the use of anti-depressants, and, if a woman is at midlife, the use of hormone replacement therapy as well. Yet, with a significant shift in a woman's psyche at midlife, many of the symptoms of depression as listed by diagnostic manuals such as the DSM-IV are understandable.

> If we persist in our modern way of treating depression as an illness to be cured only mechanically and chemically, we may lose the gifts of soul that only depression can provide...The soul apparently needs amorous sadness. It is a form of consciousness that brings its own unique wisdom. (Moore, 1992: 146)

Jung's theory for midlife development proposes that all of us at midlife, both men and women, need to face our fears of letting go of our conditioned attitudes and beliefs about how we define ourselves and how we choose to live our lives, and be willing to move in to the unknown and the experience of inner pain as we connect with aspects of ourselves repressed in the past (Vickers-Willis, 2004: 74–84). Research on women experiencing depression indicates that

> women recognized that the uncertainty of recovery was also part of the process of refusing who they had been told they should be to become someone "other". (Fullagar, 2008: 48)

If a woman chooses not to go on this journey into the unknown at midlife, she shrinks back within herself: her mind becomes ever narrower and rigid as she tenaciously holds on to societal attitudes and values she was inculcated with in the first half of her life. In contrast, with successful navigation of the challenges offered by midlife transition a woman is led to determine her own set of values and attitudes leading to an ever-expansive way of experiencing her own identity (Jung, 1985).

How does a woman navigate midlife transition? The answers lie within her. Most women at midlife do sense an inner guiding force. The proliferation of and interest by women at midlife in spiritual books, talks and workshops supports this belief. Her inner voice speaks to her from her unconscious through images, metaphors and symbols. If she shows an accepting and friendly manner to them, they will guide her on her way. When she makes time to connect with her inner world through such activities as meditation, noticing her dreams, writing, creative and leisure pursuits, or just by simply being still, research indicates she does find answers that help her find her own identity (Fullagar, 2008: 46).

Developing a greater sense of her own true nature, however, may only lead to ongoing frustration and depression if she can't create a personal world where she can be herself. This can be the midlife task women find most difficult as they struggle with creating a personal world where they can honour who they perceive themselves to be. A common thread running through women's recovery stories from depression is their desire to become more assertive, a skill that I also noted as vital if a woman is to create a personally meaningful second half of life (Ibid.; Vickers-Willis, 2002).

In her middle to late thirties a woman is typically at a stage where her life is busy. She has multiple roles: children, partners, career, parents, in-laws, siblings and other relatives, friends, children's schools and the community may be drawing on her energy and time (Strazdins & Broom, 2004). Typically, having valued herself in the first half of life drawing on the ideal of the "good woman", she now looks at all her responsibilities and feels overwhelmed and caged in by them. The demanding life she was so willing to put hours of time into no longer has the same attraction. As her inner voice gets more insistent, she looks out at this world and wonders, 'Where is there space for me?' Or perhaps, even when there is space, she finds there is something within that stops her from taking time for herself. Many women have self-denying thoughts that sabotage them when they are trying to make changes, such as "I must not be selfish", "I must not be demanding", "I am only worthwhile when I am doing things for others", "I don't deserve", are conditioned voices within her, often at an unconscious level. She needs to challenge these self-sabotaging thoughts as they discourage her from making changes and creating a life where she can be herself.

Some ignore the inner prompting for change. Others notice and remain in a state of inner dis-ease as they hold on to beliefs and attitudes that no longer serve them. Yet, anything other than honouring her Self, her inner guidance, will lead to a second half of life full of regrets and inner dissatisfaction. A life that is only half lived, resulting in ongoing lifelessness, depression and illness.

Women are socialized to create a sense of self based on "the masculine gaze", with a focus on attractiveness to the opposite sex and the ability to please others. They are also encouraged to disown their own feelings, as femininity has historically been inferiorized as weak, dependent and emotional (Jack, 1991). It can be very confrontational for a woman at midlife, and for those around her, as she acknowledges that these societal values and attitudes no longer ring true for her. This is why a crisis in her outer world, such as the end of her primary relationship, may be what it takes for a woman at midlife to re-evaluate every aspect of her life as "emotions can destabilise fixed notions of gender identity" (Fullagar, 2008: 38).

As a woman at midlife faces the break-up of a relationship that she has dedicated much of her adult life to, there will be many losses for her to grieve, both real and otherwise: her own perceptions of her physical beauty and sexual attractiveness; the possibility she may never have children; the role of motherhood as she faces "the empty nest"; her lost career opportunities and earning prospects as she anticipates competing in a youth- and male-focused work world.

As she evaluates what beliefs and attitudes have personal meaning for her now, it is normal for her to experience feelings that are part of the grief process. If she doesn't understand what feelings are normal at a time of loss and change, she can become terribly frightened as she experiences such feelings as anger, despair and depression. These feelings are there to help her to let go and then rebuild, but if she gets caught up in the fear of the experience she may get stuck and never make the necessary changes to create a personally satisfying second half of life.

She might resort to desperate defences so as not to experience these frightening feelings. She might get frantically busy, hoping that by being very active and pretending that everything is all right she can ignore the terror inside her. She might even think that she is going crazy as she experiences anxiety and depression. Other people who share her lack of understanding may also think that she has a mental illness and describe her as manic, depressed or as having a nervous breakdown, or they might see it as a hormonal problem. Yet all that has happened is that she is starting to grieve as the belief structure that has supported her in the first half of life is collapsing.

In her classic book, *On Death and Dying* (1970), Dr Elizabeth Kubler-Ross was the first person to clearly articulate the stages of grief and the emotions experienced when a loved one dies. It is now recognised that these stages and emotions equally apply when we experience any change, for in any change we experience a mini-death or loss. It is also important to acknowledge that individuals find their own unique process for grieving, and so although Kubler-Ross' stages of grief are presented one after the other, individuals can move in and out of different stages of grief without following any particular order.

The first stage of grief is disbelief and denial. For example, after a woman's long-term relationship has ended, she may say to herself "this isn't happening to me. We don't really mean it. Life will soon go back to normal." Such feelings and thoughts can give a woman time to get used to the change, but eventually she does need to move on to the next stage: bargaining. This stage is an attempt to deny the irreversibility of the situation. Loss of a significant relationship might initiate such reactions as "I can change", "I can be nicer", "we should wait until the children are older", or "we should go to counselling again". This allows time for rethinking and imagining new possibilities. Next, when she realises that the change is inevitable and that there isn't a lot she can do to go back to the old life, she experiences intense feelings of anger: "Why is this happening when we have spent so many years building a life together?" or "Why am I being treated so shabbily after years of being loyal?" During this stage she may react erratically and experience fury and anger. It is important for her to find appropriate ways to express these emotions as they allow her to move on to the next stage.

Despair and depression may now overwhelm her. She feels totally helpless. It is as if she falls into a hole. She now starts questioning every belief she has lived her life by. This is a time when sleeping and eating patterns can be deeply affected. She may not want contact with others, yet supportive friends can make a huge difference. Professional help may be needed. If she gives herself time, accepts that these feelings are normal at a time of loss, and gives herself the space to grieve, she supports herself enormously. It is important for her not to make any significant decisions during this time as she may be eager to fill the void and a hasty choice may prove unwise.

After days, weeks, months or perhaps even years of being mainly in her personal world of grieving, feelings of self-pity give way to acceptance. For some it is a gradual grieving and moving forward; for others it is as though one day they wake up and look at the world with new eyes. They can see a way forward. Their world is different. They are different. They can now let go enough to start moving on. They start to rebuild an understanding of who they are and what they want in their life based on a more conscious awareness of themselves and their world. With this understanding about what feelings are normal at a time of change and loss, a woman assists herself while in the midst of the turmoil of midlife transition by telling herself, "I'm changing. My life is changing. These feelings are normal at midlife. I'll survive. By allowing myself to experience these feelings, rather than running away from them or sedating them with anti-depressants, I will eventually create a life that suits me well." Alternatively, she may cling on in fear to old beliefs such as "I have to have a partner to be happy" or "I mustn't rock the boat", and as she does she denies herself the chance to find new ways of creating happiness and personal fulfilment for the second half of her life.

It is vital for a woman to realise that turbulent feelings at midlife are there for a reason, as they encourage her to make the necessary changes to create a second half of life centred round who she truly is. When I now look back to how I felt in my mid-thirties, I know I was experiencing lethargy as my psyche encouraged me to slow down, spend time with myself and go within to find out more about my own true nature; I felt sadness as I grieved aspects of my first half of life including all those things I now knew would never be; and I felt anger and frustration as I became restless to find ways in my life to express an increased understanding of who I was. In reporting on her study of women who had experienced depression, psychologist Simone Fullagar notes:

> All of the women talked about recovery as an ongoing process of finding ways to better understand, live with, and manage the emotions that emerged from expectations and situations. (2008: 42)

In a culture where there is no acknowledgement of midlife transition and where women's depression is formulated as a biomedical problem related to hormones and chemical imbalance or as a psychological problem related to over-emotionality and inability to cope, it is almost inevitable that women experiencing depression at midlife will be misdiagnosed by health professionals.

The often emotionally turbulent developmental transition adolescents go through as they move from childhood to early adulthood is well accepted. I wonder how long it will be before Western culture, and most importantly its health professionals, acknowledge that there is an equally important emotionally turbulent developmental transition for adults at midlife as they move from the first to the second half of life.

Bibliography

Alexander, R. *Cycles of Becoming*: CRCS Publications, 1978.

American Psychiatric Association (APA). *Diagnostic and Statistical Manual of Mental Disorders*. Fourth ed. 1992.

Boughton, S., and H. Street. "Integrated Review of the Social and Psychological Gender Differences in Depression." *Australian Psychologist* 42 no. 3 (2007): 187–97.

Butler, J. *Undoing Gender*. New York, NY: Routledge, 2004.

Campbell, J. *The Hero with a Thousand Faces*. Bollingen Series XV11. Princeton, PA: Princeton University Press, 1973.

Dante, Alighieri. *The Divine Comedy, I: Inferno*. Translated by John D. Sinclair. Oxford University Press, 1961.

Erikson, E. H. *The Life Cycle Completed: A Review*. New York, NY: W. W. Norton and Company, 1982.

Frenkel, E. "Studies in Biographical Psychology." *Character and Personality* 5 (1936): 1–34.

Fullagar, S. "Leisure Practices as Counter-Depressants: Emotion-Work and Emotion-Play within Women's Recovery from Depression." *Leisure Sciences* 30 (2008): 35–52.

Gilligan, C. *In a Different Voice: Psychological Theory and Women's Development*. Cambridge, MA: Harvard University Press, 1993.

Gutmann, D. *Reclaimed Powers: Toward a New Psychology of Men and Women in Later Life*. New York, NY: Basic Books, 1987.

Jack, D. *Silencing the Self: Women and Depression*. Cambridge, MA: Harvard University Press, 1991.

Jaques, E. "Death and the Midlife Crisis." *International Journal of Psychoanalysis* 46 (1965): 502–514.

Jung, C. G. *Memories, Dreams, Reflections*. London, England: Random House, 1961.

—. *Psychological Types*. [New ed.] London, England: Routledge & Kegan Paul, 1971.

—. *Modern Man in Search of a Soul*. London, England: Routledge & Kegan Paul, 1985.

Kegan, R. *The Evolving Self: Problem and Process in Human Development*. Cambridge, MA: Harvard University Press, 1982.

Kleiber, D., S. Hutchinson and R. Williams. "Leisure as a Resource in Transcending Negative Life Events; Self-Protection, Self-Restoration and Personal Transformation." *Leisure Sciences* 24 no. 2 (2002): 219–35.

Kubler-Ross, E. *On Death and Dying*. London, England: Tavistock Publications Ltd., 1970.

Levinson, D. J. *The Seasons of a Man's Life*. New York, NY: Knopf, 1978.

McAdams, D. P. *The Person: An Integrated Introduction to Personality Psychology*. Fort Worth, TX: Harcourt College Publishers, 2000.

—. *The Redemptive Self: Stories Americans Live By*. Oxford, England: Oxford University Press, 2006.

—. *The Stories We Live By: Personal Myths and the Making of the Self*. New York, NY: Guilford Press, 1996.

Moore, T. *Care of the Soul*. New York, NY: Harper Collins, 1992.

O'Connor, P. *Understanding Jung*. Melbourne, Australia: Reed Books, 1988.

Oliver, M. *Dream Work*. Berkeley, CA: Grove/Atlantic Inc., 1986.

Polden, J. *Regeneration: Journey through the Mid-Life Crisis*. London, England: Continuum, 2002.

Sheehy, G. *Passages for Men*. Sydney, Australia: Simon & Schuster, 1998.

—. *Pathfinders: Overcoming the Crisis of Adult Life and Finding Your Own Path to Well-Being*. New York, NY: William Morrow, 1981.

Sheehy, Gail. *New Passages: Mapping Your Life across Time*. New York, NY: Random House, 1995.

Stein, M. *In Midlife: A Jungian Perspective*. Dallas, TX: Spring Publications, 1983.

—. *Jung's Map of the Soul*. Chicago, IL: Carus Publishing Company, 1998.

Strazdins, L., and D. Broom. "Acts of Love (and Work): Gender Imbalance in Emotional Work and Women's Psychological Distress." *Journal of Family Issues* 25 no. 3 (2004): 356–78.

Vickers-Willis, R. *Men Navigating Midlife*. Sydney: Allen & Unwin, 2004.

—. *Navigating Midlife: Women Becoming Themselves*. Sydney, Australia: Allen & Unwin, 2002.

World Health Organization (WHO). "Women's Mental Health: An Evidence-Based Review." Department of Mental Health and Substance Dependence, ed. Geneva, Switzerland: WHO, 2000.

PSYCHIATRY AND THE DEPRESSED WOMAN

CAROLYN QUADRIO

Introduction

It has long been established that depression occurs more commonly—about twice as much—in women than in men (Henderson, 1995; Seeman, 1995; Wolk & Weissman, 1995). There are gender differences also in the presentation and the course of depression—with more chronicity in women—and also in treatment responses (Kornstein, 1997, 2000). No single explanation seems adequate and there are a number of factors that contribute to this phenomenon. This article provides an overview of some of the factors and also some observations about psychiatric approaches to depressed women. The separate headings employed here are rather arbitrary: it is often impossible to separate the psychological, the biological and the social.

Trauma and Abuse

There is considerable evidence that adverse experiences in childhood, especially physical and sexual abuse, play a part in the higher rates of depression in women (Bifulco et al., 2002; Chapman et al., 2004; Hill et al., 2001; Levitan et al., 1998; Mullen et al., 1988; Nolen-Hoeksema, 2001; Piccinelli et al., 2001; Weiss et al., 1999). The effects of multiple forms of childhood abuse are dose-related: life-time prevalence for depression is 14 percent in women who have suffered no abuse; 26 percent with one form of abuse, either sexual or physical; and 38 percent when both have occurred (Bifulco & Moran, 1998).

Not only does the psychological impact of childhood abuse continue into adulthood (Mullen et al., 1993), women survivors of childhood abuse are at greater risk for revictimisation in terms of physical and sexual trauma in adulthood (Arata et al., 2006; Coid et al., 2001). Their lifetime risk of rape is about 12 percent and physical violence from intimate partners—reports of violence in the previous twelve months—are between

21 and 30 percent (Mazza et al., 2001). In a study of depressed women, Dienemann et al. (2000) found a 61 percent lifetime prevalence for domestic violence and 29.3 percent for forced sex.

Biogenetic Factors

Genes are the holy grail of contemporary medical and psychiatric research and there is no dearth of genetic explanations for depression. The increased prevalence of depression in women cannot be attributed, however, to genetic loading (Merikangas et al., 1985) and there is considerable evidence that what genetic influences there are operate via stressful life events (Kendler et al., 1995; Kendler et al., 1997). As Kendler argues that there is no simple relationship between a gene and a complex disorder or trait: "The impact of individual genes on risk for psychiatric illness is small, often nonspecific, and embedded in complex causal pathways" (2005, 1243). Such evidence does not dampen the enthusiasm of researchers, for example, Nemeroff and Vale (2005) acknowledge that "intensive" research efforts have been expended in the search for the genetic underpinnings of mental illness, citing the human genome inventory, chromosome mapping and DNA sequencing as perhaps providing the "genetic basis of mental illnesses"; they agree that trauma in early life, including sexual and physical abuse, alters neural circuits but conclude by hoping for "molecular targets for new drug development, biological risk factors, and predictors of treatment response" (2005: 5). Clearly their orientation is towards a pharmaceutical solution, but perhaps "intensive efforts" might be better aimed at making women and children safer.

The previous holy grail of medical/psychiatric research was the hormonal one, starting with theories of wandering wombs, ideas of depression in women being related to their reproductive functions dominated well into the twentieth century. The effect of estrogen on depression, however, remains a controversial area (Studd et al., 2004). There is little evidence that menopause generally or oestradiol in particular causes depression (Avis et al., 2001; Nicol-Smith, 1996), although hormonal changes may "contribute" to dysphoric mood at that time (Freeman et al., 2004). Neither is there direct evidence that hormonal imbalance causes postpartum depression; here Miller (2002) concludes that biological changes are significant but appear to operate in the context of environmental stress or insufficient social support; again the suggested future direction is biological: that hormone therapy may play a role in treatment and prevention.

This is not to argue that genetic factors and hormonal changes do not contribute to emotional and psychological disturbances in women—elsewhere I have argued extensively against any dichotomous nature/nurture arguments and have proposed that only a complex "feminist biopsychosocial model" can provide an adequate account (Quadrio, 2001) —but what is constantly in evidence in medical and psychiatric research is the privileging of biomedical factors over psychosocial. That bias is at least in part if not mostly explained by the investment of the pharmaceutical industry which has much to gain from the continuing pathologisation of the female condition (Russell 1995).

Psychiatry too has a long and unedifying history of pathologising women and of a somewhat morbid preoccupation with female physiology. There was an attempt in the late 80's to introduce premenstrual syndrome (PMS) into the third revision of the diagnostic manual (DSM) as "late luteal phase dysphoric syndrome", a condition said to be characterised by depression, irritability and hostility and as seriously interfering with work, social activities and relationships with others. Powerful action from a group of feminist clinicians was successful in defeating this proposal on the basis that there was inconclusive evidence for a syndrome and that if it did exist it appeared to affect 40 to 60 percent of the female population so could hardly be considered abnormal (Ritchie, 1989).

Research continues, however, with every aspect of the menstrual cycle examined, as if somehow the mystery of womankind will be discovered there—even the "seasonality" of PMS symptoms has been studied (Maskall et al., 1997). There are reports of seasonality in domestic violence too (Michael & Zumpe, 1986) as well as in other forms of male violence (Sivarajasingam et al., 2002; Tiihonen et al., 1997), yet there is nothing like the same interest in cyclical changes in the male psyche as with the female. It seems that women have a long way to go before shaking off the association between lunar and lunacy.

Again this is not an argument against any hormonal influences on a woman's psyche—it is not a question of pitting biomedical models against psychosocial ones—rather it is a matter of integrating all dimensions and of asking why it is chiefly female sexuality that is problematised. The eternal fascination with cyclical changes in female physiology might seem to imply that male sexuality is constant and unproblematic; instead it is one of the major threats to society and to the mental health of women and children. Data on physical and sexual violence against women and children and the impact on their mental health—universally—attest to the enormity of the problem (Pinheiro, 2006; United Nations, 1994, 2006).

Sociocultural/Political/Economic Factors

While contemporary psychiatry claims to be based on a biopsychosocial model (Engel, 1980; Sadler, et al., 1992) that takes into account all these dimensions of psychological disturbances, in reality it is greatly skewed towards the biological (Silove, 1990; McLaren, 1998; Read, 2005). Even though it might claim to be multidimensional the biopsychosocial perspective generally fails to incorporate those historical and political dimensions that are critical to understanding the position of women. A truly multidimensional approach to the nexus between gender and psychiatry must account for the historical and universal reality of women's inferior social, economic and political status (Ortner, 1974; Rosaldo, 1974; United Nations, 2006). In developed nations the gender gap is closing but remains nonetheless a reality for many women; in most parts of the world the oppression and marginalisation of women is a fact of life. Their exposure to abuse and trauma is also a fact of life—some data on this has been reviewed above—it is a critical reflection of the sociocultural, political and economic status of women. If there are some universalisable truths about women, they include that women suffer more (civilian) violence, abuse and harassment, and more poverty, and they have less power and status than men (Kendler et al., 2001; Nolen-Hoeksema, 2001; Piccinelli et al., 2001; Vahtera et al., 2006). In that context it would seem hardly surprising that they also suffer more depression (and anxiety and post traumatic disorders).

Psychological Factors

An important aspect of the higher prevalence of depression in females is the propensity to internalise distress—one that is apparent from early childhood (Golombok & Fivush, 1994). This process of internalisation may account for the preponderance of female sufferers of both anxiety and depression (Harris, 2001); in fact there is evidence that these are not separate disorders at all and there is an argument for collapsing them into one group of "distress and fear disorders" (Clark & Watson 2006); they might also be regarded as internalising disorders.

The internalising process in females is magnified by their willingness to seek medical or psychiatric intervention and therefore to become "cases" (van Hook, 1999). Women are more likely to "diagnose themselves" (Garton, 1988); they are more likely to seek treatment, regarding it as an appropriate way to deal with their problems. In contrast, men are more likely to externalise their distress; they are also less inclined to help seeking behaviour and hence less likely to present to doctors or mental health professionals (Jorm, 1995). In externalising their negative emotions men are more likely to manifest risk taking and antisocial behaviours, which may lead them to the prison or the mortuary rather than the clinic. They are less likely to take medication and more likely to self medicate with drugs or alcohol and so may obscure their issues with depression or anxiety (Page & Andrews 1996). Similarly, men who are pathological gamblers also have a high incidence of depression (Blaszczynski & Silove, 1996).

To what extent the internalising/externalising spectrum is a psychological phenomenon versus a socially acquired/learned behaviour is a question that is beyond the scope of this paper but one I have addressed in more detail elsewhere (Quadrio, 2001).

Women are more sensitive to interpersonal stressors and this too bears on their propensity to depression (Kendler et al., 2001) and speaks to another important—and different—aspect of femaleness: women are relational and affiliative. Any consideration of female psychology—or its disturbances—must take account of gender difference. It is not only depression that affects women differently compared to men—there is almost no category in the DSM system that does not show gender difference, including: disturbances of personality and of mood, the anxieties, phobias and post traumatic conditions and the psychoses. As a generality females manifest more internalising behaviours and react with more fear and/or sadness where males manifest more externalising behaviours and react with more anger;[1] this is true from early childhood and has its origins in prenatal behaviour (Cicchetti & Cohen 1995).

These differences must be understood developmentally. The classic developmental models—Erikson (1969); Levinson et al. (1978); Vaillant (1977); and Piaget (1965)—were mostly unisex; woman-centred models emerged only after second wave feminism in the 1970s, *inter alia*, with Miller (1976), Dinnerstein (1977) and Chodorow (1978). I have argued that a woman-centred model must allow for three aspects of psychosexual development that are most distinctively different for females compared with males: affiliation and an orientation of other-directedness; maternity or maternalism and continuity in the mother/daughter relationship; and alterity, the position of women as "other" (Quadrio, 2001).

---

[1] There are 378 separate psychiatric diagnoses listed in the DSM and, almost without exception, each disorder shows a sex distribution which could be predicted in terms of stereotypic gender differences (Quadrio, 2001).

A Feminist Biopsychosocial Model

Gender differences operate at every level, biologically, psychologically, socially and politically; females and males develop differently out of differentiated genetic material and in the context of a gender differentiated world; they function differently and, psychiatrically, they present differently (Quadrio, 2001). A feminist biopsychosocial model accounts for this multidimensionality: as gendered beings we develop within complex hierarchically and gender organised environmental influences that are historically determined. Femaleness has been constructed as the result of a complex sociohistorical process that constitutes it as subordinate to and less than maleness. This evolution does not proceed in one direction: bidirectionality allows for feedback and feedforward processes such that genetic material can be altered by environmental influences (Gottlieb, 1996; Seeman, 1995).

Along with many other feminist clinicians, I have argued that a predominantly biomedical model pathologises women and does not address the complex social, historical, economic and political forces that are responsible for their universally socially disadvantaged position. At the same time I have argued against a polarisation of these views and for a multidimensional approach. There is an extreme feminist view, that women's madness is entirely a product of patriarchal oppression (McLellan, 1995; Russell, 1995), but this simply inverts the biomedical view; it cannot account adequately for the mental health problems of socially advantaged women in developed nations and it does not recognise that mind and brain are inseparable (although not identical) and that the function of one must always be reflected in changes in the other. Similarly there is nothing in the material world that either exists or operates independently of its environment.

The strong relationship between women's psychiatric disorders and their experiences of abuse and violence (Stewart & Robinson, 1994) begs a sociopolitical solution; yet even in this context a dualistic approach is problematic. It is not, as argued by Russell (1995), a question of either accepting the psychiatric system of diagnosing post-abuse syndromes or pursuing a "social/political account". To describe a rape victim as suffering from a post traumatic stress disorder does not minimise the reality of the rape but it does acknowledge the profound psychological injury that is also suffered. These are complex situations and do not have one dimensional solutions. There is much available in psychobiological, neuropsychiatric and biogenetic research that may provide a better understanding of psychopathology and of the significance of gender differences in psychiatric disorders—provided that it remains grounded in a social and political account. The social and political implications of psychiatric disorder are profound and, at their worst, can lead to violations of civil liberties and atrocities against human rights (Bloch, 1997). Yet a feminist psychiatry is a possibility and even a necessity. Rather than dismiss psychiatry as oppressive to women, we might work towards the project of a politically informed and gender sensitive psychiatry; this would rest on a complex and multidimensional understanding of psychiatric disorders.

Psychiatry and the Depressed Woman

The "prototypical" patient in psychiatry is the depressed middle-aged woman (Coyne, 1987). There was a time when she might be locked away, either at home or in an asylum; with the advent of the psychoanalytic era in psychiatry she would spend years on the couch, exploring the vagaries of her relationship with her mother or perhaps her illicit desire for her father; today she will almost certainly be taking antidepressants and she may also be learning to challenge her distorted cognitions. This is certainly great progress from the asylum days but perhaps there is still cause for discomfort: it appears that the female brain needs pharmaceutical help to correct its chemical imbalances and needs therapies as well to correct its cognitive distortions, its thinking errors. There is too much here that seems to echo past theories of hormonal imbalances and defective female brains. We know that much of the psychological distress of women is related to the trauma of abuse and of interpersonal violence (Bifulco et al., 1991; Mullen et al., 1988; Stewart & Robinson, 1994); without doubt these traumas affect brain function but the treatments referred to here are not always offered with that perspective. Too many drugs are prescribed too readily, and especially to women, for what are often chiefly psychosocial issues.

Women and Drug Therapies

Feminist and other critics of psychiatry (Breggin, 1993; Russell, 1995; Healy, 2003) have expressed concern about the frequency with which women are prescribed psychotropic medications. The manufacture of new antidepressants is a booming billion dollar industry; and then there are pharmaceutical treatments for the side effects of these drugs—for example Viagra may be prescribed to combat the diminished sexual drive that often results from taking antidepressants (Nurnberg et al., 2008). But what if the woman's depression is related to childhood sexual abuse? And what if there is sexual violence in her marriage? What then of treatment with Viagra?

In developed countries it is unlikely that women can be discouraged from medical treatment of their psychological problems—at least not any time soon. They are not simply victims of clever marketing; many well informed women insist on taking psychotropic medication. In that case there are other issues that need consideration. There are significant gender differences in the metabolism of drugs and many have been developed and promoted without ever being trialed on women (Hamilton et al., 1995; Jensvold et al., 1996). As with much science, studies are based upon "normal" subjects—men—while women are often excluded because of the vagaries of female physiology. Yet women are prescribed more psychotropic medication than are men.

This is not an argument against any use of psychotropic medication but it is an argument against the brain blaming approach to psychiatry (Valenstein, 2000). There are two entirely different approaches to the use of psychotropic medications: they may be provided for symptomatic relief while the more fundamental problems in the person's life are being addressed; or, they may be offered as the definitive treatment—as chemical correction of chemical brain imbalance—the depression-is-like-diabetes approach—an approach that promises a life time of antidepressant dependence. Evidence suggests that this is not the best approach. Before the advent of the newer (SSRI) antidepressants, the definitive study on the merits of medication versus psychotherapy was that of Elkin et al. (1989): imipramine (one of the older, tricyclic antidepressants) with clinical management gave the best outcome but interpersonal therapy (psychotherapy) was also superior to either placebo or clinical management alone. Since then there have been numerous studies comparing the newer SSRIs with psychotherapy or with a combined approach; it is difficult to be confident of this research since so much of it is underwritten by the pharmaceutical industry, but de Jonghe et al (2004) —who seem to be independent researchers—were unable to demonstrate a convincing improvement when adding antidepressants to psychotherapy.

Gender and Prescribing Practices

In my 2001 review of data on the treatment practices of women and men psychiatrists it was apparent that more prescribing was done by the men; the women provided more relational therapies, especially with female patients. I proposed that male psychiatrists relate to female patients with less empathy and are more likely to invoke biological models to explain their problems and more inclined to objectify and to pathologise them and to prescribe the quicker, less expensive treatment option of a prescription.

Gender and Electroconvulsive Therapy

In the same study there were marked differences with respect to ECT, with men psychiatrists providing three times as much to a predominantly (80 percent) female patient population. The national Australian data showed similarly that male psychiatrists provide most of this treatment (more than 90 percent), including to some child patients; no women psychiatrists provided ECT to minors.

About one third of the (mostly female) patients receiving ECT were aged over 60; this is usually explained as that older people are vulnerable to severe depression but are less tolerant of medication. Jorm and Henderson (1989) found similar distributions but even allowing for an over-representation of women in this older population and the fact that in the over 60s the sex ratio of women and men presenting with depression is about 3:2 (Seeman, 1995), their data showed an excess of what would be predicted; they questioned whether this was due to a higher incidence of more psychotic and organic disorders in the elderly or whether it relates to psychiatrists' perceptions that psychological treatments are inappropriate for the elderly and have a poorer prognosis and are less suitable for psychotherapy. I have suggested that there are also issues of both sexism and ageism—or of "othering" (Wilkinson & Kitzinger, 1996). Psychotherapy requires a level of empathy which is dependent upon certain commonalities of experience in terms of age, sex, class and culture. It is likely that patients who are constituted as "other" are less likely to be engaged in the "talking therapies" and more likely to receive biological treatments. It is not surprising that the more like each other they are, the better two people will understand each other (Nadelson, 1993). My data suggested that the less privileged are more likely to be treated by a male psychiatrist; this includes women from non-English speaking backgrounds. This combination of difference in both gender and in socioeconomic status widens the chasm of understanding that is possible and in my view predisposes to a more biological formulation of the person's difficulties and a more biological approach to treatment.

Abuse in Psychiatric Treatment

Even in seeking treatment for depression women are still at risk of abuse. Some 7 to 10 percent of male and 1 to 3 percent of female psychiatrists and psychologists have sexual contact with their clients; offenders are mostly senior clinicians with excellent professional training and background (Gabbard, 1989; Gartrell et al., 1989; Leggett, 1994; Quadrio, 1996; Schoener et al., 1989). My experience in this is based on assessments of more than sixty women patients. Most originally sought help because of depression; about half had a history of childhood abuse or neglect or serious family dysfunction. Their profiles are similar to those reported by other researchers: most were well informed; most were in paid employment, many in a professional role; about one half were themselves health care professionals, nurses, social workers, trainee psychiatrists, professional counsellors or psychologists.

The experience of sexual abuse by a trusted clinician is universally and seriously traumatising; these women suffered a worsening of their original problem, severe depression and many developed post-traumatic stress disorder. Family and marital breakdown were common. They were left feeling guilt and shame and anger, a sense of hopelessness and pervasive mistrust. In subsequent therapies, some were so depressed that they had to be hospitalised, sometimes over a period of several years. Most failed to respond to a variety of pharmacological interventions and three failed to respond to ECT. Severe and persistent suicidal feelings were common, and three were involuntarily committed because they were dangerously suicidal.

Conclusion

Women are at risk of abuse and trauma throughout their lives and even when seeking treatment they are at risk. These stark realities together with the problems arising from their position of social, political and economic disadvantage are sufficient to account for much of their despair. Delineating the neuropsychological pathways from lived experience to expressed mood remains a fascinating project but should not be allowed to obscure women's shared and their individual histories.

My thanks to Carrol Besseling, who kindly assisted with the editing.

Bibliography

Anderson, M. A., P. M. Gillig and M. Sitaker. "Why Doesn't She Just Leave?: A Descriptive Study of Victim Reported Impediments to her Safety." *Journal of Family Violence* 18 no. 3 (2003): 151–155.

Arata, C. M. "Child Sexual Abuse and Sexual Revictimization." *Clinical Psychology: Science and Practice* 9 no. 2 (2006): 135–64.

Avis, N. E., S. Crawford, R. Stellato and C Longcope. "Longitudinal Study of Hormone Levels and Depression among Women Transitioning through Menopause." *Climacteric* 4 no. 3 (2001): 243–249.

Bifulco, A., G. W. Brown and Z. Alder. "Early Sexual Abuse and Clinical Depression in Adult Life." *The British Journal of Psychiatry* 159 (1991): 115–22.

Blaszczynski, A., and D. Silove. "Pathological Gambling: Forensic Issues. *Australian and New Zealand Journal of Psychiatry* 30 (1996): 319–325.

Breggin, P. R. *Toxic Psychiatry*. London, England: Harper Collins, 1993.

Chodorow, N. *The Reproduction of Mothering*. Berkeley, CA: University of California Press, 1978.

Cicchetti, D. and D. J. Cohen. *Developmental Psychopathology Volumes I and II*. New York, NY: John Wiley and Sons. 1995.

Clarkin, J. F., J. W. Hull, J. Cantor and C. Sanderson. "Borderline Personality Disorder and Personality Traits: A Comparison of SCID-II BPD and NEO-PI." *Psychological Assessment* 5 no. 4 (1993): 472–476.

Clark, L. A., and D. Watson. "Distress and Fear Disorders: An Alternative Empirically Based Taxonomy of the 'Mood' and 'Anxiety' Disorders. *The British Journal of Psychiatry* 189 (2006): 481–483.

Coid, J., A. Petruckevitch, G. Feder, W. Chung, J. Richardson, S. Moorey. "Relation between Childhood Sexual and Physical Abuse and Risk of Revictimisation in Women: A Cross-Sectional Survey. *The Lancet* 358 no. 9280 (2001): 450–454.

Coyne, J. C. "Depression, Biology, Marriage and Marital Therapy." *Journal of Marital and Family Therapy* 13 (1987): 393–407.

de Jonghe, F., M. Hendricksen, G. van Aalst, S. Kool, V. Peen, R. Van, E. van den Eijnden and J. Dekker. "Psychotherapy Alone and Combined with Pharmacotherapy in the Treatment of Depression." *The British Journal of Psychiatry* 185 (2004): 37–45.

Dienemann, J., E. Boyle, D. Baker, W. Resnick, N. Wiederhorn and J Campbell. "Intimate Partner Abuse among Women Diagnosed with

Depression." *Issues in Mental Health Nursing* 21 no. 5 (2000): 499–513.

Dinnerstein, D. *The Mermaid and the Minotaur*. New York, NY: Harper and Row, 1977.

Engel, G. L. "The Clinical Application of the Biopsychosocial Model." *American Journal of Psychiatry* 137 (1980): 535–44.

Eisenstein, H. *Contemporary Feminist Thought*. London, England: Unwin Paperbacks, 1984.

Elkin, I., T. Shea and J. Watkins. "NIMH Treatment of Depression Collaborative Research Program: General Effectiveness of Treatments." *Archives of General Psychiatry* 46 (1989): 971–82.

Erikson, E. *Childhood and Society*. Harmondsworth, England: Penguin Books, 1969.

Freeman, E. W., M. D. Sammel, L. Liu, C. R. Gracia, D. B. Nelson and L. Hollander. "Hormones and Menopausal Status as Predictors of Depression in Women in Transition to Menopause." *Archives of General Psychiatry* 61 (2004): 62–70.

Gabbard, G. O. *Sexual Exploitation in Professional Relationships*. Washington D. C.: American Psychiatric Press, 1989.

Garton, S. *Medicine and Madness*. Sydney, Australia: New South Wales University Press, 1988.

Gartrell, N., J. Herman, S. Olarte, M. Feldstein and R. Localio. "Prevalence of Psychiatrist–Patient Sexual Contact." In G. O. Gabbard, ed., *Sexual Exploitation in Professional Relationships*. 3–13. Washington D.C.: American Psychiatric Press, 1989.

Griffing, S., D. F. Ragin, S. M. Morrison, R. E. Sage, L. Madry and B. J. Primm. "Reasons for Returning to Abusive Relationships: Effects of Prior Victimization. *Journal of Family Violence*, 20 no. 5 (2005): 341–48.

Golombok, S., and R. Fivush. *Gender Development*. New York, NY: Cambridge University Press, 1994.

Gottlieb, G. "A Systems View of Psychobiological Development." In D. Magnusson, ed., *The Lifespan of Individuals: Behavioural, Neurobiological and Psychosocial Perspectives*. 76–103. New York, NY: Cambridge University Press, 1996.

Hamilton, J. A., M. F. Jensvold, E. D. Rothblum and E. Cole, eds. *Psychopharmacology from a Feminist Perspective*. New York, NY: Harrington Park Press, 1995.

Harris, T. "Recent Developments in Understanding the Psychosocial Aspects of Depression." *British Medical Bulletin* 57 (2001): 17–32.

Healy, D. *The Antidepressant Era.* Boston, MA: Harvard University Press, 2003.

Henderson, S. C. "The Mental Health of Australians: Can Informative Data be Found?" *Australian and New Zealand Journal of Psychiatry* 59 (1995): 6–13.

Hendrick, V., L. L. Altshuler and R. Suri. "Hormonal Changes in the Postpartum and Implications for Postpartum Depression." *Psychosomatics* 39 (1998): 93–101.

Jensvold, M. F., U. Halbreich and J. A. Hamilton. *Psychopharmacology and Women.* Washington, D.C.: American Associated Press, 1996.

Jorm, A. F., ed. *Men and Mental Health.* Canberra, Australia: National Health and Medical Research Council, 1995.

Kendler, K. S. "'A Gene for...': The Nature of Gene Action in Psychiatric Disorders." *American Journal of Psychiatry* 162 (2006): 1243-1252.

Kendler, K. S., and L. Karkowski-Shuman. "Stressful Life Events and Genetic Liability to Major Depression: Genetic Control of Exposure to the Environment?" *Psychological Medicine,* 27 (1997): 539–47.

Kendler, K. S., R. C. Kessler, E. E. Walters, C. MacLean, M.C. Neale, A. C. Heath and L. J. Eaves. "Stressful Life Events, Genetic Liability, and Onset of an Episode of Major Depression in Women." *American Journal of Psychiatry* 152 (1995): 833–42.

Kendler, K. S., L. M. Thornton and C. A. Prescott. "Gender Differences in the Rates of Exposure to Stressful Life Events and Sensitivity to Their Depressogenic Effects. *American Journal of Psychiatry* 158 (2001): 587–93.

Kornstein, S. "Gender Differences in Depression: Implications for Treatment." *Journal of Clinical Psychiatry* 58 no. S15 (1997): 12–8.

—. "Gender Differences in Chronic Major and Double Depression." *Journal of Affective Disorders* 60 no. 1 (2000): 1–11.

Leggett, A. "A Survey of Australian Psychiatrists' Attitudes and Practices Regarding Physical Contact with Patients." *Australian and New Zealand Journal of Psychiatry* 28 (1994): 488–97.

Levinson, D. J., C. N. Darrow, E. B. Klein, M. H. Levinson and B. McKee. *The Seasons of a Man's Life.* New York, NY: Alfred A. Knopf, 1978.

Livesley, W. J., K. L. Jang and P. A. Vernon. "Phenotypic and Genetic Structure of Traits Delineating Personality Disorder." *Archives of General Psychiatry,* 55 (1998): 941–48.

Maskall, D. D., R. W. Lam, S. Misri, D. Carter, A. J. Kuan, L. N. Yatham and A. P. Zis. "Seasonality of Symptoms in Women with Late Luteal

Phase Dysphoric Disorder." *American Journal of Psychiatry* 154 (1997): 1436–441.

Mazza, D., L. Dennerstein, C. V. Garamszegi and E. Dudley. "The Physical, Sexual and Emotional Violence History of Middle-Aged Women: A Community-Based Prevalence Study. *Medical Journal of Australia* 175 (2001): 199–201.

McGoldrick, M. "Women through the Family Life Cycle." In M. McGoldrick, C. Anderson and F. Walsh, eds., *Women in Families*. 200–26. New York, NY: W. W. Norton and Company, 1989.

McLaren, N. "A Critical Review of the Biopsychosocial Model." *Australian and New Zealand Journal of Psychiatry* 32 no. 1 (1998): 86–92.

Merikangas, K. R., M. M. Weissman and D. L. Pauls. "Genetic Factors in the Sex Ratio of Major Depression." *Psychological Medicine* 15 no. 1 (1985): 63–9.

Michael, R. P., and D. Zumpe. "An Annual Rhythm in the Battering of Women." *The American Journal of Psychiatry* 143 (1986): 637–40.

Miller, J. B. *Toward a New Psychology of Women*. Harmondsworth, England: Penguin Books, 1976.

Miller, L. J. "Postpartum Depression." *Journal of American Medical Association* 287 (2002): 762–65.

Mullen, P. E., S. E. Romans-Clarkson, V. A. Walton and G. P. Herbison. "Impact of Sexual and Physical Abuse on Women's Mental Health." *Lancet* 16 no. 1 (1988): 841–45.

Mullen, P. E., J. L. Martin, J. C. Anderson, S. E. Romans and G. P. Herbison. "Childhood Sexual Abuse and Mental Health in Adult Life." *The British Journal of Psychiatry* 163 (1993): 721–32.

Nemeroff, C. B., and W. W. Vale. "The Neurobiology of Depression: Inroads to Treatment and New Drug Discovery." *The Journal of Clinical Psychiatry* 66 no. 7 (2005): 5–13.

Nicol-Smith, L. "Causality, Menopause, and Depression: A Critical Review of the Literature." *British Medical Journal* 313 (1996): 1229–232.

Nolen-Hoeksema, S. "Gender Differences in Depression." *Current Directions in Psychological Science*, 10 (2001): 173.

Nurnberg, H. G., P. L. Hensley, J. R. Heiman, H. A. Croft, C. Debattista and S. Paine. "Sildenafil Treatment of Women with Antidepressant-Associated Sexual Dysfunction: A Randomized Controlled Trial." *Journal of American Medical Association* 300 no. 4 (2008): 395–404.

Office of the United Nations High Commissioner for Human Rights. *Declaration on the Elimination of Violence against Women.* Geneva, Switzerland: United Nations, 1994.

Ortner, S. "Is Female to Male as Nature is to Culture?" In M. Rosaldo and L. Lamphere, eds., *Woman, Culture and Society.* 67–8. Stanford, CA: Stanford University Press, 1974.

Page, A., and G. Andrews. "Do Specific Anxiety Disorders Show Specific Drug Problems?" *Australian and New Zealand Journal of Psychiatry* 30 (1996): 410–14.

Piaget, J. *The Moral Judgement of the Child.* New York, NY: The Free Press Paperback Edition, 1965.

Pinheiro, P. S. *The Consequences of Violence against Children: United Nations Secretary General's Report on Violence against Children.* Geneva, Switzerland: ATAR Roto Presse SA, 2006.

Piccinelli, M., and G. Wilkinson. "Gender Differences in Depression." *The British Journal of Psychiatry* 177 (2000): 486–92.

Quadrio, C. "Sexual Abuse in Therapy: Gender Issues." *Australian and New Zealand Journal of Psychiatry* 30 (1996): 124–33.

—. *Women Working and Training in Australian Psychiatry.* Glebe, Australia: Bookhouse, 2001.

Read, J. "The Bio-Bio-Bio Model of Madness." *The Psychologist* 18 (2005): 596–97.

Ritchie, K. "The Little Woman Meets the Son of DSM-III." *The Journal of Medicine and Philosophy* 14 (1989): 695–708.

Roberts, R. R., ed. *Handbook of Domestic Violence Intervention Strategies: Policies, Programmes and Legal Remedies.* Oxford, England: Oxford University Press, 2002.

Rosaldo, M. Z. "Woman, Culture, and Society: A Theoretical Overview." In M. Z. Rosaldo and L. Lamphere, eds., *Women, Culture, and Society.* 17–42. Stanford, CA: Stanford University Press, 1974.

Russell, D. *Women, Madness and Medicine.* Cambridge, England: Polity Press, 1995.

Sadler, J. Z., and Y. F. Hulgus. "Clinical Problem-Solving and the Biopsychosocial Model." *American Journal of Psychiatry* 149 (1992): 1315–323.

Schoener, G. R., J. H. Milgrom, J. C. Gonsoriek, E. T. Luepker and R. M. Conroe, eds. *Psychotherapists' Sexual Involvement with Clients: Intervention and Prevention.* Minneapolis, MN: Walk-In Counselling Center, 1989.

Seeman, M. V., ed. *Gender and Psychopathology.* Washington D. C.: American Psychiatric Press, 1995.

Silove, D. "Biologism in Psychiatry." *Australian and New Zealand Journal of Psychiatry* 24 (1990): 461–64.

Sivarajasingam, V., J. Shepherd, K. Matthews and S. Jones. "Trends in Violence in England and Wales, 1995–2000: An Accident and Emergency Perspective." *Journal of Public Health Medicine* 24 (2002): 219–226.

Stewart, D. E., and G. E. Robinson. "Violence against Women." In J. M. Oldham and M. B. Riba, eds., *Review of Psychiatry, Vol. 14.* 261–82. Washington D. C.: American Psychiatric Press, 1994.

Studd, J., and N. Panay. "Hormones and Depression in Women." *Climacteric* 7 no. 4 (2004): 338–46(9).

Tiihonen, J., P. Räsänen and H. Hakko. "Seasonal Variation in the Occurrence of Homicide in Finland." *The American Journal of Psychiatry* 154 (1997): 1711–17.

United Nations. *Ending Violence against Women: From Words to Action.* Study of the Secretary General of the United Nations. Geneva, Switzerland: United Nations, 2006.

United Nations Department of Public Information. *Women and Violence.* Geneva, Switzerland: United Nations, 1996.

Vahtera, J., M. Kivimäki, A. Väänänen, A. Linna, J. Pentti, H. Helenius and M. Elovainio. "Sex Differences in Health Effects of Family Death or Illness: Are Women More Vulnerable than Men?" *Psychosomatic Medicine* 68 (2006): 283–91.

Vaillant, G. E. *Adaptation to Life.* Boston, MA: Little, Brown and Company, 1977.

Valenstein, E. S. *Blaming the Brain: The Truth about Drugs and Mental Health.* New York, NY: Free Press, 2000.

Van Hook, M. P. "Women's Help-Seeking Patterns for Depression." *Social Work in Health Care* 29 no. 1 (1999): 15–34.

Weissman, M. M. "Gender Differences in the Rates of Mental Disorders." In S. Thaul and D. Hostra, eds., *Assessing Future Research Needs: Mental and Addictive Disorders in Women.* 8–13. Washington D. C: Institute of Medicine, 1991.

Wilkinson, S., and C. Kitzinger. *Representing the Other: A Feminism and Psychology Reader.* London, England: Sage, 1996.

Wolk, S. I., and M. M. Weissman. "Women and Depression: An Update." In J. M. Oldham and M. B. Riba, eds., *American Psychiatric Press Review, Vol. 14.* 227–60. Washington D. C.: American Psychiatric Press, 1995.

CONTRIBUTORS

Belinda Cody was awarded a Master's in Creative Arts Therapy from RMIT University in Melbourne, Australia, in 2006. She has worked as a multi-modal arts therapist with clients as diverse as youths in prison, Vietnam War veterans with PTSD, people with dementia, and also patients in palliative care in the Aged Care sector. She runs community arts therapy groups for both men and women, and has also taught and supervised post-graduate students on the MCAT course at RMIT University. She is a professional member and office bearer of ACATA, and a candidate in the Professional Doctorate program at MIECAT, Melbourne.

Kim Davis holds a Master's in Applied Science and Social Ecology, and a Degree and Certificates in Adult Education, Counselling and Coaching. Kim is also a qualified Dru Yoga teacher/therapist and has been teaching and researching Dru Yoga and depression since 2005. She is a member of the International Yoga Therapist Association, the International Meta Coaching Association and the International Association of Positive Psychology. Kim is currently working with indigenous communities in Darwin, Australia. www.anahata-services.com

Isabelle Ellis, RN, RM, MPH & TM, MBA, PhD, is a Professor at the Combined Universities Centre for Rural Health, University of Western Australia. Isabelle's research interest is in facilitating the link between generalist health care practitioners and specialists using telecommunications and IT technologies. Isabelle was co-author Karen Noonan's lecturer during her undergraduate degree and was inspired by her story and her storytelling to assist in the development of the chapter "Porphyria Makes me Depressed".

Elizabeth Ettorre holds a PhD in Sociology from the London School of Economics. She is currently Professor of Sociology at the School of Sociology and Social Policy, University of Liverpool, UK. Her work focuses on women and health. In this area, she has developed a specific interest in reproduction, drugs, embodiment and depression. Her most recent publications are: Culture, Bodies and the Sociology of Health (2010); Revisioning Women and Drugs: Gender Power and the Body (Palgrave 2007) and Reproductive Genetics, Gender and the Body (2002).

Sabin Fernbacher, PhD, is the Women's Mental Health Consultant at the Northern Area Mental Health Service in Melbourne, Australia. She has held a number of positions for over twenty years focusing on sexual assault, family violence, homelessness and mental illness. Her doctoral research focused on mental health policy and the level of guidance provided to mental health services about family violence and sexual abuse. She feels passionate about creating possibilities for change towards increasing service responses for people with mental illness who have experienced trauma. Contact details: sabin.fernbacher@mh.org.au

Christine Hodge is the manager of the Primary Mental Health Team and the Youth Early Psychosis Program at the Northern Area Mental Health Service in Melbourne, Australia. Christine has a Master's in Psychology and is currently studying Health Management. She has worked in mental health for over twenty years in nursing, psychology and mental health management roles. Her interest focuses on early intervention in mental health and consultation, liaison and collaborative partnerships between mental health services and community primary care services. Contact details: christine.hodge@mh.org.au

Iffat Hussain holds a Master's in Physiology from the University of Karachi, Pakistan, and obtained her second Master's in International Services Management from the Netherlands, Stenden University. She has worked for UNICEF projects and in several other community-based projects with other NGOs. She is the author of *Problems of Working Women in Karachi, Pakistan*, published by Cambridge Scholars Publishing. Her articles on culture and social issues have been published in various magazines and newspapers. Contact details: iffat_hussain123 @hotmail.com

Irmeli Laitinen, PhD, is a psychoanalytic psychotherapist and a group analyst. She currently works as a Psychotherapist in the National Health Service in England. She completed her PhD, "Depression in / by / for Women: Agency, Feminism and Self-help in Groups" at the University of Helsinki in August 2008. She has been consistently involved in women's mental-health issues and was one of the founding members of the Women's Therapy Centre in Helsinki, Finland.

Nancy Moodley is a Clinical Psychologist at the Provincial Spinal Rehabilitation Centre, Phoenix Assessment and Therapy Centre, Department of Health and Department of Behavioural Medicine, Nelson R. Mandela School of Medicine, University of KwaZulu-Natal, Durban, South Africa. She is currently completing a PhD in the area of spinal cord injury and neuropsychology at the Nelson R. Mandela School of Medicine, UKZN.

Magnolia Bahle Ngcobo obtained her Master's degree in clinical psychology from the University of Port Elizabeth. She is employed as a clinical psychologist and lecturer by the KwaZulu Natal department of Health and University of KwaZulu Natal. She is currently working on her PhD at the University of KwaZulu Natal.

Karen Noonan, RN, was diagnosed with Porphyria in 2001. At that time very little information was known about this condition, which is why she decided to research the disease. She discovered that there were many misconceptions and a lack of understanding of this disease, and she wanted to learn to manage her own health. She has presented papers on porphyria at national and international conferences. She has also recently started her own health-coaching business, which looks at promoting self-management of chronic conditions, and she plans to do further research in this area. She is a Registered Nurse and will soon be finished with her post-graduate studies.

Tracie O'Keefe, DCH, ND, is a Clinical Hypnotherapist, Psychotherapist, Counsellor and Naturopath. She is originally from London and now based in Sydney. Dr. O'Keefe is the clinical and educational director of the Australian Health & Education Centre in Glebe, Australia, and the author of several books on sex, gender and sexuality, as well as *Self-Hypnosis for Life: Mind, Body & Spiritual Excellence*. Contact details: www.tracieokeefe.com

Basil J. Pillay is a Professor at and Head of Department of Behavioural Medicine at the Nelson R Mandela School of Medicine at the University of KwaZulu-Natal, and Chief Clinical Psychologist for the Hospital Services of the KwaZulu-Natal Provincial Administration in Durban, South Africa. He is an internationally recognized academic and clinician, representing his discipline on national and international bodies as well as serving on several scientific committees. He is a past President of the Psychological Society of South Africa (PsySSA).

Carolyn Quadrio is a Conjoint Associate Professor in Psychiatry at the University of New South Wales, Australia. She practices and teaches in forensic and child and family psychiatry, particularly in cases of sexual abuse and intra-familial violence. She is well-known for her research on women in psychiatry and sexual abuse of patients in therapy.

Shari Read has a PhD in social psychology with a research interest in how the social and political environment can affect the way people express their beliefs and attitudes. As a therapist Shari specializes in women's reproductive mental health during pregnancy and the postnatal period. She runs a national independent childbirth preparation program, Birth Skills, and supports women and their families through natural and mind/body therapies during early parenthood.

Debra Rickwood is Professor of Psychology at the Centre for Applied Psychology. She is a community psychologist who researches in the areas of young people's help-seeking behaviour; factors affecting mental health and wellbeing, including alcohol and other drug use, the promotion, prevention and early intervention for mental health, recovery from mental illness, and health service evaluation.

Robyn Vickers-Willis has thirty years' experience as a practicing psychologist. Since 2000, the focus of her work has been to research and write about the importance of adults growing in consciousness from midlife and beyond. She is currently completing a PhD at the University of Melbourne titled "Midlife Matters in Australia". She is the author of *Navigating Midlife: Women becoming Themselves, Men Navigating Midlife* and *Navigating the Empty Nest: Re-creating Relationships*, published by Wayfinder Publishing. Contact details: www.navigating midlife.com